SpringerBriefs in Ethics

Springer Briefs in Ethics envisions a series of short publications in areas such as business ethics, bioethics, science and engineering ethics, food and agricultural ethics, environmental ethics, human rights and the like. The intention is to present concise summaries of cutting-edge research and practical applications across a wide spectrum.

Springer Briefs in Ethics are seen as complementing monographs and journal articles with compact volumes of 50 to 125 pages, covering a wide range of content from professional to academic. Typical topics might include:

- Timely reports on state-of-the art analytical techniques
- A bridge between new research results, as published in journal articles, and a contextual literature review
- A snapshot of a hot or emerging topic
- In-depth case studies or clinical examples
- Presentations of core concepts that students must understand in order to make independent contributions

More information about this series at https://link.springer.com/bookseries/10184

Marcus Smith • Seumas Miller

Biometric Identification, Law and Ethics

Marcus Smith
Charles Sturt University
Canberra, ACT, Australia

Seumas Miller
Charles Sturt University
Canberra, ACT, Australia

TU Delft
Delft, The Netherlands

University of Oxford
Oxford, UK

The research was conducted under the auspices of: (i) the European Research Council's Advanced Grant programme as part of the grant entitled, "Global Terrorism and Collective Moral Responsibility: Redesigning Military, Police and Intelligence Institutions in Liberal Democracies" (GTCMR. No. 670172) (Principal Investigator: Professor Seumas Miller) and (ii) the Australian Research Council's Discovery Grant program as part of the grant entitled, "Intelligence and National Security: Ethics, Efficacy and Accountability" (DP180103439).

ISSN 2211-8101   ISSN 2211-811X (electronic)
SpringerBriefs in Ethics
ISBN 978-3-030-90255-1   ISBN 978-3-030-90256-8 (eBook)
https://doi.org/10.1007/978-3-030-90256-8

© The Author(s) 2021. This book is an open access publication.
Open Access This book is licensed under the terms of the Creative Commons Attribution 4.0 International License (http://creativecommons.org/licenses/by/4.0/), which permits use, sharing, adaptation, distribution and reproduction in any medium or format, as long as you give appropriate credit to the original author(s) and the source, provide a link to the Creative Commons license and indicate if changes were made.
The images or other third party material in this book are included in the book's Creative Commons license, unless indicated otherwise in a credit line to the material. If material is not included in the book's Creative Commons license and your intended use is not permitted by statutory regulation or exceeds the permitted use, you will need to obtain permission directly from the copyright holder.
The use of general descriptive names, registered names, trademarks, service marks, etc. in this publication does not imply, even in the absence of a specific statement, that such names are exempt from the relevant protective laws and regulations and therefore free for general use.
The publisher, the authors, and the editors are safe to assume that the advice and information in this book are believed to be true and accurate at the date of publication. Neither the publisher nor the authors or the editors give a warranty, expressed or implied, with respect to the material contained herein or for any errors or omissions that may have been made. The publisher remains neutral with regard to jurisdictional claims in published maps and institutional affiliations.

This Springer imprint is published by the registered company Springer Nature Switzerland AG
The registered company address is: Gewerbestrasse 11, 6330 Cham, Switzerland

Acknowledgement

The research was conducted under the auspices of: (i) the European Research Council's Advanced Grant program as part of the grant entitled "Global Terrorism and Collective Moral Responsibility: Redesigning Military, Police and Intelligence Institutions in Liberal Democracies" (GTCMR. No. 670172) (Principal Investigator: Professor Seumas Miller) and (ii) the Australian Research Council's Discovery Grant program as part of the grant entitled "Intelligence and National Security: Ethics, Efficacy and Accountability" (DP180103439).

Contents

1	**The Rise of Biometric Identification: Fingerprints and Applied Ethics**	1
	1.1 Overview of Biometric Identification	1
	1.2 The First Biometric: Fingerprint Identification	3
	1.3 Applied Ethics	7
	1.4 Collective Moral Responsibility	9
	1.5 Fingerprinting: Key Ethical Issues	14
	1.6 Conclusion	17
	References	17
2	**Facial Recognition and Privacy Rights**	21
	2.1 Facial Recognition	21
	2.1.1 Databases	23
	2.1.2 CCTV Integration	24
	2.1.3 Social Media Integration	27
	2.2 Ethical Principles	29
	2.2.1 Privacy	29
	2.2.2 Security and Public Safety	33
	2.3 Conclusion	35
	References	36
3	**DNA Identification, Joint Rights and Collective Responsibility**	39
	3.1 DNA Identification	39
	3.2 Legal Issues	41
	3.3 Genomics and Forensic Genealogy	44
	3.4 Ethical Analysis	47
	3.4.1 Joint Rights to Genomic Data	51
	3.4.2 Collective Moral Responsibility to Assist Law Enforcement	52
	3.5 Conclusion	53
	References	54

4	**Biometric and Non-biometric Integration: Dual Use Dilemmas**	57
	4.1 Data Systems and Integration	57
	4.1.1 Metadata	60
	4.1.2 Smartphone Applications	64
	4.1.3 Social Media	66
	4.2 Ethical Analysis	68
	4.2.1 Dual Use Ethical Dilemmas	69
	4.3 Conclusion	75
	References	76
5	**The Future of Biometrics and Liberal Democracy**	79
	5.1 Future Biometrics	79
	5.2 Biometric Futures	81
	5.2.1 Social Credit Systems	81
	5.2.2 Technology-Based Regulation	85
	5.3 Liberal Democracy	88
	5.4 Conclusion	91
	References	93
Index		97

About the Authors

Marcus Smith is Associate Professor in Law at Charles Sturt University and Adjunct Professor of Law at the University of Canberra. He holds a PhD in law from the Australian National University. He has published widely on technology law, regulation and ethics. His previous books include: *Technology Law* (Cambridge University Press, 2021), *Biometrics, Crime and Security* (Routledge, 2018) and *DNA Evidence in the Australian Legal System* (LexisNexis, 2016).

Seumas Miller has research appointments at Charles Sturt University, TU Delft and the University of Oxford. He is the principal investigator on a European Research Council Advanced Grant on counter-terrorism ethics, and is the author of more than 200 academic articles and 20 books, including *The Ethics of Cybersecurity* (with Terry Bossomaier) (Oxford University Press, 2021) and *Dual Use Science and Technology, Ethics and Weapons of Mass Destruction* (Springer, 2018).

Chapter 1
The Rise of Biometric Identification: Fingerprints and Applied Ethics

Abstract In the late nineteenth century, it became understood that the patterns on the skin of the fingers were unique and could be used for identification purposes, leading to the development of biometric identification (Smith M, Mann M, Urbas G. Biometrics, crime and security. Routledge, 2018). The ease with which fingerprints can be accessed and recorded, and the ease with which they transfer to surfaces and objects, made them ideal for law enforcement purposes. Today, in digital form, fingerprints and other biometric identification techniques, notably DNA profiles and facial recognition technology, are a widely used means of identification across a range of applications, from accessing personal devices, to banking, border security and law enforcement. However, these uses have raised a raft of ethical or moral (we use these terms interchangeably) concerns, some of the more important of which we discuss in this work.

In the first chapter, we discuss general aspects of biometric identification, before focusing on fingerprint identification, including its reliability as form of evidence. Secondly, we provide an overview of applied ethics; and outline a key theoretical notion, relevant to many of the issues discussed throughout the later chapters: collective responsibility. Finally, we analyse the ethical risks and benefits associated with the technique of fingerprint identification.

Keywords Biometric identification · Fingerprint identification · Criminal investigation · Applied ethics · Collective responsibility · Joint action

1.1 Overview of Biometric Identification

Biometrics refers to the measurement of physical aspects of the human body. This can include patterns of the skin or blood vessel networks under the skin; patterns in the genetic code; facial appearance, such as the distance between features such as the eyes, nose or mouth; and behavioural traits, such as gait (Smith et al., 2018). For identification purposes, in addition to being a physical feature capable of being measured, biometrics must be unique between individual humans, able to be efficiently verified, and unchanging over time. They must also be capable of being digitalised through an algorithm and converted to a format that can be integrated with automated database storage and searching.

Biometric identification can be contrasted with other methods of identification, such as keys, identification cards and passwords. The obvious distinction being that a biometric is a reference to part of the individual themselves, rather than an object carried on the person, or password held in their mind. Biometric identification has been described as: rather than being something that an individual *knows* or *has*, it is something that they *are* (Hopkins, 1999).

The first known application of a form of biometric identification took place in Ancient Egypt, for the purpose of ensuring that food provided by the state was shared equitably among those legitimately eligible to receive it. A system was developed to record distinctive physical and behavioural characteristics of workers, along with their name, age and place of residence, to ensure individuals did not obtain more than their allocated allowance. A significant development occurred in the mid-nineteenth century, when Czech scientist Jan Evangelista Purkinje (1787–1869) established that fingerprints were unique (Ashbourn, 2000). The classification system for fingerprints was developed by Sir Francis Galton (1882–1911) and Sir Edward Henry (1850–1931). The Henry classification system provided a method to classify fingerprints and exclude potential match candidates, establishing fingerprinting as a basis for individual identification and the foundation of fingerprint databases. This was quickly adopted by law enforcement agencies, led by Scotland Yard, and databases were later developed in collaboration with the private sector, throughout the twentieth century (Allen et al., 2005).

Fingerprint identification became the central identification tool in criminal investigation until the mid-1980s, when it was overshadowed by the arrival of DNA profiling; however, it remains relevant today (Smith, 2016). Over the past decade, facial recognition technology has been an area of advancement within the field of biometrics, alongside a range of new DNA profiling techniques. The past decade has also seen the expansion of biometrics in society, from personal devices such as laptops and smartphones, to building access and banking services, it is rapidly replacing traditional methods of access and identity verification such as keys and personal identification numbers.

Biometrics can be used for one-to-many searching, where an unknown individual's biometric profile is compared with a database of profiles to identify them, such as in a criminal investigation context. It can also be used for one-to-one verification of identity, determining whether an individual is who they purport to be. A live profile can be compared with a template stored in the computer system or identification document, such as a passport or licence. Biometric identification can also be used is to identify individuals on a watch-list, such as by screening closed circuit television footage with facial recognition technology (Smith et al., 2018).

Individual biometrics have strengths and weaknesses, depending on the context in which they are used. Seven criteria have been accepted as key indicators of the suitability of biometric features: universality, distinctiveness, permanence, collectability, performance, acceptability, and resistance to circumvention (Jain et al., 2006) (Table 1.1). For example, fingerprinting or facial recognition may be selected over gait analysis at passport control; but when analysing television footage to identify a suspect, gait analysis may be preferred because it can be assessed from a greater distance and obtaining fingerprints from such a large group of people would not be feasible. Ideally, facial recognition could be combined with gait analysis to provide a higher degree of accuracy.

1.2 The First Biometric: Fingerprint Identification

The technique of fingerprint identification, in both analogue and digital forms, is based on differences within the standard patterns of the ridges. These can be classified into a series of arches, loops and whorls. The centre of a pattern is referred to as the core, and points of deviation referred to as the delta. The points of discontinuity in a fingerprint, where a ridge branches or ends, are known as minutiae. Approximately 30 minutiae are used in the fingerprinting technique. Fingerprinting has advanced significantly with digitalisation in the twenty-first century. Optical scanners and algorithms are now used to record, digitally retrieve and match fingerprint data; in contrast with the initial manual, card-based system. Automated fingerprint databases of hundreds of millions of people have now been established. These are fully automated, or only require human input at the final stage to distinguish between highly similar fingerprints as part of a list of close matches to an unknown suspect in a law enforcement investigation (Moses et al., 2010).

Since the mid-2000s, fingerprint identification has been widely used outside law enforcement, with the first major development being the integration of biometric fingerprint identification (along with facial recognition) into passports and border control systems. This was made a requirement for foreign nationals and visa applicants in many countries, including the United States in 2004, Japan and the United Kingdom in 2008, the European Union in 2011, and Canada in 2013 (Canadian Government, 2017). It is also widely used across Africa, the Middle East and Asia. Non-government organisations, such as the Office of the United Nations High Commissioner for Refugees (UNHCR), also use fingerprint identification to identify refugees in aid programs, using portable, battery powered devices in remote settings (Lodinová, 2016). Perhaps the largest fingerprint identification database is the government administered Aadhaar database in India, which includes more than 1.2 billion people for public administration purposes (Saferstein, 2015).

Over the past decade, fingerprint identification has been widely used outside law enforcement and government. This includes for employee attendance and building access control; and in personal devices such as smartphones and laptops. The introduction of fingerprint scanning capabilities into smartphones has provided an opportunity to apply fingerprint identification into a broader range of commercial applications – it is now common for personal banking to be undertaken online with biometric fingerprint identification. Other developing applications of fingerprint identification include within the handpiece of a firearm to ensure that it can only be

Table 1.1 Key indicators of the suitable biometric features

Universality	Distinctiveness	Permanence	Collectability	Acceptability	Performance	Resistance to circumvention
The biometric should be present in all individuals.	The biometric feature should be sufficiently different to distinguish between individuals.	The biometric feature should be unchanged over the individual's life.	The degree of ease of collecting and measuring the biometric.	The extent to which an individual or society accepts the use of the biometric feature as a means of identification.	The degree of accuracy and the speed of the system.	The extent to which the system can be bypassed or defeated.

used by the registered owner. It is being deployed by government in relation to firearms for police and military personnel to improve safety (Simonetti et al., 2017).

Biometrics are arguably a more accurate and convenient means of recording employee attendance than traditional methods such as punch clocks or swipe cards, and as costs have decreased, they have become increasingly common. In the case *Jeremy Lee v. Superior Wood Pty Ltd*,[1] a sawmill company implemented fingerprint scanners to record employee attendance. When one employee refused to provide his fingerprint and was subsequently dismissed, litigation ensued resulting in litigation over the fairness of their dismissal on that basis. On appeal it was held that because biometrics were classified as sensitive information under privacy law, consent was required to collect this information. Without it, the direction to use the scanners was not a 'lawful and reasonable direction' and Mr Lee's failure to follow the direction was not a valid reason for dismissal. This issue for employers can be addressed by making the collection of biometric data a condition of employment that would need to be accepted prior to commencing work (Holland & Tham, 2020).

Biometric fingerprint databases, known as Automated Fingerprint Identification Systems (AFIS), were first established in the late 1990s, and these continue to be a primary method of establishing identity in law enforcement and border protection contexts. Law enforcement systems include a standardised ten-print holding of fingerprints obtained under controlled conditions from a suspect during the course of an investigation, or following arrest; as well as latent fingerprints (formed from traces of sweat, oil or other substances on the surface of the skin) obtained from crime scenes or items physical evidence. Latent fingerprints are typically of lower quality and may only include a partial print (Milne, 2013).

A range of biometric fingerprint databases have been established around the world. The United States introduced the Integrated Automated Fingerprint Identification System (IAFIS) in 1999, transitioning to the multimodal Next Generation Identification (NGI) system in 2011, which also includes photographs, facial templates and criminal history and intelligence data. The NGI is operated by the Federal Bureau of Investigation (FBI) and provides services to federal, state and local law enforcement and national security agencies throughout the United States (FBI, 2017). The national fingerprint database in the United Kingdom is known as IDENT1. A key difference in this jurisdiction is that the database was developed as a joint venture between the Home Office and the defence technology company Northrop Grumman in 2004. It provides a link between law enforcement agencies across England, Wales and Scotland, as well as records in the Police National Computer (Northrop Grumman, 2017). In Australia, the national biometric fingerprint database has operated since 2001. The National Automated Fingerprint Identification System (NAFIS) provides Australian law enforcement, security and border agencies, with a centralised national database for finger and palm print images (ACIC, 2020). Data sharing arrangements have been established between these countries, as well as Canada and New Zealand (Canadian Government, 2017).

---

[1] [2019] FWCFB 2946.

The digitisation of fingerprint identification through automated databases has led to a significant increase in positive identifications and linkages between individuals and physical evidence at other crime scenes, enhancing the efficiency of investigations. An evaluation of the fingerprint database in the United Kingdom examined the collection of fingerprint evidence in relation to volume crimes, such as burglary and motor vehicle thefts, demonstrating a greater capacity to identify suspects as well as faster case outcomes (Saferstein, 2015). Despite new forms of biometrics being developed, fingerprint identification continues to play an important and growing role in law enforcement. Figures from Australia indicate a significant expansion in database searches over the past decade. For example, in the 2007–2008 financial year, there were approximately 300,000 searches for fingerprints on the national database, and by the 2018–2019 financial year this had increased to more than 1.5 million searches (ACIC, 2019).

The legal system plays an important role in evaluating and regulating evidence such as biometric fingerprints – this form of identification evidence can have a significant bearing on the outcome of proceedings. As discussed, crime scene examiners may obtain 'latent' fingerprints or palm prints on objects, which can link a defendant to a crime. Over the past century courts have routinely admitted fingerprint evidence.[2] Evidence of a fingerprint match would be presented by the investigating police officer with specialised knowledge of fingerprinting techniques, or a forensic scientist who collected and compared the prints.[3]

Identification evidence is circumstantial, and the probative value of a fingerprint match must be assessed in the context of the other evidence in a criminal trial; but it will be of greatest value to the prosecution if there is no innocent explanation for its presence at a crime scene. Obtaining fingerprints at a crime scene and comparing them using a database and the specialist knowledge of a forensic scientist is regulated by forensic procedures legislation. Collecting fingerprints from a suspect is regulated by criminal procedure legislation – generally, there must be reasonable grounds for believing that requiring a suspect to provide their fingerprints would be necessary for identifying the person responsible for a sufficiently serious offence, and if that requirement is satisfied, they may be obtained without the suspect's consent.[4]

The comparison of fingerprints involves the identification of numerous minutiae within the print.[5] The more points that are compared, and the greater the degree of similarity, the more persuasive the inference that can be draw regarding identity. The comparison of fingerprints differs from other forms of biometrics, such as DNA identification in that it does not involve the calculation of a match probability that two samples came from the same individual. It is based on human judgment in

---

[2] *Parker v R* [1912] HCA 29; (1912) 14 CLR 681, Griffith CJ at 683, cited in *R v Mitchell* [1997] ACTSC 93; (1997) 130 ACTR 48 (18 November 1997).
[3] See, for example, *DPP v Watts* [2016] VCC 1726 (23 November 2016).
[4] Section 3ZJ, *Crimes Act 1914* (Cth).
[5] *JP v Director of Public Prosecutions (NSW)* [2015] NSWSC 1669 (11 November 2015), [36].

making a visual comparison, aided by a database and algorithm, rather than a statistical calculation (Edmond, 2015).

Expert evidence law provides that a witness with specialised knowledge must be able to explain how identification evidence provides a sound basis for the conclusions they draw about the evidence.[6] To the extent that any of the evidence is unclear, the defence may seek to have it excluded, or ask for the jury to be cautioned regarding the weight they accord it.[7] Judges must consider that a jury hearing, for example, that the defendant's fingerprints were matched to a crime scene using a police database, may infer that the defendant has a criminal history. The defence could seek to exclude evidence as unfairly prejudicial or seek to have the judge to warn the jury against making an adverse inference on that basis.

1.3 Applied Ethics

Issues in applied ethics, including many public policy issues, have a value dimension as well as a scientific dimension. The value dimension is in need of systematic analysis and illumination by way of moral theories and perspectives. Here it is not simply a matter of philosophical theory being mechanically applied to specific problems; rather there is a complex interplay between theoretical perspectives, on the one hand, and specific ethical intuitions and concrete scientific data, on the other. For example, whether or not biometric identification constitutes an infringement of the right to privacy, is partly a matter of figuring out what is important about privacy (the ethical theory of privacy) as well as knowing the scientific facts about the particular biometric in question and the uses to which it is put by, for instance, law enforcement. Further, it may well be a matter of balancing the moral weight to be given to privacy against the benefits delivered by these databases in the specific contexts in question. On the other hand, it may well call for creative thinking of a kind that would enable us to possess integrated databases without necessarily infringing the right to privacy. For example, such databases might be able to be designed in such a way that access was available only to certain persons under highly restricted circumstances, e.g. law enforcement officials possessed of a judicial warrant in the circumstance of a very serious crime. That is, our agreed ethical perspective on this issue could be designed-into the technology or the institutional, including legal, arrangements (van den Hoven et al., 2017).

The philosophical theory itself operates at a number of levels of abstraction. There are high level theoretical claims, such as the principle of maximizing the satisfaction of the greatest number or seeking to benefit the least advantaged

---

[6] Leading authorities on specialized knowledge under UEL s79(1) are *Makita (Australia) Pty Ltd v Sprowles* [2001] NSWCA 305 (14 September 2001); *HG v The Queen* [1999] HCA 2; 197 CLR 414; and *Honeysett v The Queen* [2014] HCA 29; 253 CLR 122.

[7] In *JP v Director of Public Prosecutions (NSW)* [2015] NSWSC 1669 (11 November 2015); *Dasreef Pty Ltd v Hawchar* [2011] 243 CLR 588.

(Alexandra & Miller, 2009a). But there are also lower level philosophical theories of specific values, e.g. an ethical theory of scientific freedom, or of a specific occupational role, e.g. an ethical theory elaborating the moral purpose and characteristic virtues of a criminal investigator or of a forensic scientist (Miller & Gordon, 2014). These lower-level normative or value theories operate within specific institutional, occupational and technological settings; they are context dependent. As such they grow out of, and are highly sensitive to, specific situations and problems.[8]

Much of the philosophical work on ethics undertaken in universities in the English-speaking world in the last century was concerned with higher order abstract theory, as opposed to lower order context dependent theory. However, it has become clear that lower order context dependent theory is back on the agenda under the heading of applied ethics. Moreover, arguably, higher order abstract theory in so far as it is purely formal (value formalism) is of little assistance in the solution of practical ethical problems. Consequentialism and formalist deontological theories are species of value formalism. (Consequentialism is, roughly speaking, the theory that one should always act in such a way as to maximise the good consequences of one's action; neo-Kantian formalist deontological accounts are erected on a principle of universalizability, i.e. only perform an action in a situation if you can consistently will everyone to perform the action in that situation.) Here we must distinguish between value formalism and substantive ethical theories. Bernard Gert offers a substantive ethical theory in this sense (Gert, 2004; Alexandra & Miller, 2009b). According to Gert there are ten moral rules, which fall into two groups. The rules in both groups instruct us not to act in ways which will cause the five basic harms rational persons want to avoid, death, pain, disability, loss of freedom, and loss of pleasure. The first five moral rules are: Do not kill; Do not cause pain; Do not disable; Do not deprive of freedom; Do not deprive of pleasure. These rules prohibit those kinds of actions that *directly* cause these harms. The second five rules are: Do not deceive; Keep your promises; Do not cheat; Obey the law; Do your duty. These rules prohibit those kinds of actions that *indirectly* cause the five basic harms. Arguably, Gert's list both omits some basic moral principles, and includes some that ought not to be included. Perhaps the two most obvious omissions from the list are 'Do not steal or damage other people's property' and 'Do not defraud'.

Moreover, Gert was apparently wrong to include as a basic rule that we should obey the law since perhaps there is a moral obligation to obey *specific* laws and *specific* legal systems, but only because those laws/legal systems embody the moral rules and/or achieve collective goods not otherwise obtainable. On this account legal systems or laws as such do not generate moral obligations, even presumptive

---

[8]This need to relativise moral theories, perspectives and principles to institutional and technological context does not imply relativism, i.e. the theory that moral statements are not objectively true. The proposition that killing is wrong stands in need of relativisation. In general, it is morally wrong to kill another human being. However, in some contexts, e.g. in a situation of self-defence, it is morally permissible. However, from the fact that moral principles need to be relativised to context, it does not follow from this that the moral claims implicit in such relativisation are not objectively true (Alexandra & Miller, 2009a Ch. 2).

moral obligations that can be overridden. So the obligation to obey the law is entirely unlike the obligation to keep one's promises. Other things being equal, making a promise creates a moral obligation. Naturally, some promises – such as a promise to kill innocent people – do not create obligations, and some promises that do create moral obligations can be overridden in certain circumstances. However, other things being equal, the fact that there is an extant legal system prescribing a particular set of acts and omissions does not entail that there is an obligation to obey those laws; rather it all depends on the laws in question, or so it could be argued. At any rate, in this work we will be making some suggestions in relation to what particular laws there ought to be in relation to different biometric technologies and their uses.

To return to substantive ethical theories: they provide an ethical framework that can usefully inform practical ethical decision-making. For this reason, it is important to utilize substantive theories and, in particular, some of their constitutive moral principles, e.g. do not deprive persons of their freedom. However, in doing so further analysis of often called for in respect of the content of these principles, e.g. the concept or, better, concepts of freedom in play. By contrast, it would seem that value formalist theories are in themselves simply too abstract to provide ethical guidance; at best they rule out certain combinations of action on the grounds of inconsistency (e.g. actions that fail the universalizability test) or unhelpfully state the obvious (e.g. 'Always take into account the consequences of your actions'). Naturally, this inadequacy of formalist theories can be addressed by providing in some other way this missing content, e.g. by drawing up a list of the good consequence to be pursued. However, this manoeuvre simply draws attention to the need for a substantive ethical theory, e.g. a theory that specifies the goods or content-laden principles in question. But the lack of such as substantive ethical theory is precisely what we do not have, and what formalist theory cannot give us. Moreover, once we have the substantive theory, there is hardly any role left for formalist theory in relation to practical ethical decision-making, or so we suggest.

1.4 Collective Moral Responsibility

The development of biometric technology, such as fingerprinting, by scientists and others, and its uses by individuals within government agencies and law enforcement, e.g. for criminal investigations, is a complex undertaking involving multiple organizations and numerous individuals. Accordingly, the activities engaged in and their outcomes are a matter of collective responsibility and, since these activities and outcome are often morally significant, collective moral responsibility. However, the notion of collective moral responsibility is itself complex, especially as it applies to such a network of interconnected activities as this.

The notion of collective moral responsibility that we will be using in this work is that of joint moral responsibility (Miller, 2001a Ch. 8, 2006, 2010 Ch. 4). Collective moral responsibility is a species of moral responsibility and contrasts, in particular, with individual moral responsibility. However, the notion of moral responsibility, whether individual or collective, contrasts with a number of other notions.

First, we need to distinguish moral responsibility (including collective moral responsibility) from causal responsibility. A person or persons can inadvertently cause a bad outcome without necessarily being morally responsible for so doing. For example, a careful and competent fingerprint expert who is obeying all the relevant regulations and best practice procedures might, nevertheless, incorrectly judge that there is a match between the fingerprints of a suspect and the fingerprints found at the crime scene leading to the arrest of an innocent person because the fingerprint sample he used was the wrong one due to an error in the chain of custody of evidence.

Second, we can distinguish moral responsibility from what can be referred to as natural responsibility. Moral responsibility typically requires not only causal responsibility but also an intention to cause good or evil (or at least the knowledge that one's action will or may well cause good or evil) and an intention that is itself under one's control. On the other hand, one is not necessarily *morally* responsible for one's actions under one's control since such action might not have any moral significance. If a fingerprint expert makes himself a cup of coffee then under normal conditions he is responsible for doing since the action is entirely under his control; however, arguably, he is not *morally* responsible for doing so, given the action of making a cup of coffee has no moral significance.

Third, we need to distinguish moral responsibility from institutional responsibility, e.g. legal responsibility. An investigator might be morally responsible for breaking her promise to a suspect without being legally responsible, or otherwise institutionally responsible, for so doing.

As is the case with individual responsibility we can distinguish between collective moral responsibility, on the one hand, and collective causal, collective natural and collective institutional responsibility, on the other hand. Collective moral responsibility is the moral responsibility that attaches to the members of both structured and unstructured groups of human persons for their morally significant actions and omissions. Organizations, e.g. security agencies, are structured groups and their members can be held collectively morally responsible for the outcomes of their joint actions, e.g. the reduction of crime.

According to the theory of collective responsibility as joint responsibility, at least one of the central senses of collective responsibility is responsibility arising from joint actions (and joint omissions (Miller, 2001b)). Roughly speaking, a joint action can be understood thus: two or more individuals perform a joint action if each of them intentionally performs an individual action but does so with the (true) belief that in so doing each will do their part and they will jointly realise an end which each of them has and which each has interdependently with the others (a collective end) (Miller, 1992, 1995, 2001a Ch. 2). Thus, the members of a major serious crime investigation team investigation a murder, comprised of investigators, forensic experts and so on might identify and arrest an offender or, perhaps, offenders (Miller, 2014, 2015). Since the realization of this end is the result of the interdependent action of individual actions of the investigators (e.g. those who interviewed

1.4 Collective Moral Responsibility

suspects, those who collected fingerprints), forensic experts (e.g. those who searched an automated fingerprint database and verified a match to a suspect), et al, it is a joint action and the end realized is a collective end. Moreover, since the identification and arrest of those who have committed serious crimes is morally significant, the members of the investigation team in question can be held to be collectively, i.e. jointly, morally responsible for this outcome (and as morally praiseworthy).

On this view of collective responsibility as joint responsibility, collective responsibility is ascribed to individuals. Each member of the group is individually morally responsible for his or her own contributory action, and (at least in the case of most small scale joint action – see below) each is also individually (fully or partially – see below) responsible for the aimed at outcome, i.e. the realised collective end, of the joint action. (We note that an outcome of a joint action might not be aimed at and, if so, it is not a constitutive element of a successful joint action, i.e. it is not the realized collective end of the joint action.) However, each is individually responsible for the realized collective end, *jointly with the others*; hence the conception is relational in character. Thus, in our above criminal investigation example, a member of the forensic team who collected fingerprints at the crime scene is ultimately responsible jointly with the other members of the investigation team (including the other forensic experts) for identifying the offenders because she performed her contributory action in the service of that collective end; the same point holds for each of the other members of the criminal investigation team. And, to reiterate, if the joint action had no moral significance then the participants would have had joint *natural* responsibility for their action but not joint, i.e. collective, *moral* responsibility for it. However, since the joint action in question is a morally significant action then, as mentioned above, the members of our forensic team are jointly (collectively) *morally* responsible for the outcome.

We note that on the theory of collective responsibility as joint responsibility it is possible that while each participant in a morally significant joint action makes a causal contribution to the aimed at outcome of the joint action, none of these contributing actions considered on its own is either necessary or sufficient for this outcome. Suppose that in a murder investigation, the forensic team provides multiple pieces to forensic evidence, e.g. fingerprints of the suspect at each of a number of connected crime scenes, including at the murder location, on threatening letters sent to the victim prior to the crime etc. None of these sets of fingerprints on it is own is either necessary or sufficient to secure the conviction of the offender, let us assume, however each set adds evidential weight to the case against the offender. Therefore, each of the members of the forensic team has some responsibility jointly with other members of the investigation team (including the other members of the forensic team) for the conviction. That is, each has a share of the collective moral responsibility for the outcome; a share jointly held with the others.

Notice that each of the members of the forensic team has only partial moral responsibility (held jointly with the others); none has full moral responsibility. This is often so in instances of joint action in which the contributing action of each is neither necessary nor sufficient for the outcome and almost always so in epistemic (or knowledge-based) joint action; and, therefore, in forensic work. However, we should note that it is not necessarily so in cases of kinetic joint action of a serious criminal nature, i.e. it is by no means necessarily true of the criminal actions which members of forensic teams investigate. Suppose that in our murder investigation example there were six offenders. Assume the six men simultaneously (deliberately and without moral justification) stabbed a seventh (innocent) man, and each does so having as an end to kill their victim. However, each knows that his one act of stabbing will only wound the victim, and that four stabs wounds taken together are necessary and sufficient to kill the victim. We further note that on this theory it is possible that in such scenarios – scenarios in which each participant makes a causal contribution which is neither necessary nor sufficient for the outcome – each participant is *fully* morally responsible (jointly with the others) for the outcome. Consider, for instance, our stabbing scenario. Firstly, each of the six men is individually fully morally responsible for the stab wound he inflicted. Secondly, the six men are jointly morally responsible for killing the man, i.e. they are jointly responsible for murder. Significantly, in relation to this joint responsibility, each of the six is *fully* morally responsible (jointly with the other five) for the murder (and, assuming there was sufficient evidence, each would in all likelihood be held criminally responsible for murder).

What of large-scale morally significant joint actions and omissions, such as the creation of a national database of fingerprints in the service of the collective good of security (Miller, 2010 Ch. 2, 2018)? These introduce a range of issues which are often not present in small scale, morally significant joint actions and omissions. For one thing, large-scale cases often involve hierarchical organizations and hence the potential for those in subordinate positions having diminished moral responsibility. For another thing, the extent of the contribution to the outcome of a joint action or omission can vary greatly from one participant to another. Indeed, some of those who make a causal contribution to a joint action – and especially to large-scale joint actions – might, nevertheless, not be genuine participants in that joint action because in performing their contributory action they were not aiming at the outcome constitutive of the joint action; some did not have its collective end as their end. On the theory of collectively responsibility as joint responsibility, the members of a number of forensic teams (together with members of other teams such as members of computer database teams who input data etc.) can be ascribed collective moral responsibility, at least in principle, for the national fingerprint database to the extent that they acted jointly with one another, (i.e. members of a given team with other members of that team, and the membership of one team with the membership of other teams[9]) in ways that led to its creation. Here the network of joint actions could be quite wide and complex without involving (either causally or in terms of their intentions, ends or responsibilities) all, or even most, members of all forensic teams, computer database teams, etc. Moreover, some joint actions or omissions are likely to be of greater moral significance than others, and some individual contributions,

---

[9] This notion of one team acting jointly with other teams involves a multi-layered structure of joint action. See Miller, 2001a, pp. 173–5, 2010, pp. 48–50, 2018.

1.4 Collective Moral Responsibility

e.g. those of the managers, of greater importance than others, e.g. those of lower echelon employees.

It is important to note here that not only is each agent individually (naturally) responsible for performing his contributory action, each is responsible by virtue of the fact that he intentionally performs this action (and his intention is under his control and connects to his action in the right way), and the action is not intentionally performed by anyone else. Of course, the other agents (or agent) *believe* that he is performing, or is going to perform, the contributory action in question. But mere possession of such a belief is not sufficient for the ascription of responsibility to *the believer* for performing the individual action in question. So, what are the agents *collectively* (naturally) responsible for? As already mentioned, the agents are collectively (naturally) responsible for the realization of the (collective) *end* that results from their contributory actions.

Consider each member of the above-mentioned major crime investigation team (Miller, 2014, 2015). Assume that while each investigator who (say) interviewed a suspect and each forensic expert who scrutinized some fingerprints, made a direct or indirect contribution to the ultimate outcome, i.e. the identification and arrest of the offenders, nevertheless, some of these actions were redundant or otherwise not causally necessary for the outcome. For instance, some initial suspects were eliminated because their fingerprints did not match those at the crime scene yet their elimination was not, as it turned out, necessary for the outcome. Therefore, the actions of a *subset* of the criminal investigation team was sufficient for the outcome; so although the actions of each and every member of the investigation team made a contribution, the actions of some of the members were not necessary (or, obviously, sufficient) to realize the collective end. Evidently, as already noted above, in joint actions (as opposed to joint omissions), while each single constitutive individual action needs to make a contribution, none needs to be causally or otherwise necessary to realize the relevant collective end.

This theoretical point has an important implication for the ascription of collective (i.e. joint) moral responsibility to participants in morally significant, large-scale joint actions, in particular, since typically in large-scale joint actions no contribution of a single participant taken on its own is necessary in order to realize the collective end of the joint action. Specifically, it is now possible, at least in principle, to ascribe collective, i.e. joint, moral responsibility to participants in morally significant, large-scale joint actions, such as a major crime investigation (Miller, 2001a Ch. 5, 2010 Ch. 1, 2014, 2015). The fact that in a large-scale joint action the action of each participant taken on its own is not necessary to realize the collective end of the joint action is not, given this theoretical point, a barrier to the ascription of moral responsibility to each participant (jointly with the others) for the realization of this collective end. Note that it does not follow from this that each participant in a large-scale joint action is *fully* morally responsible (jointly with the others) for the realization of the collective end of the joint action, e.g. the arrest of a large number of offenders in a major crime investigation. Indeed, this is unlikely given that the causal contribution of each in large-scale joint actions is often very small and the commitment of each to the collective end correspondingly very weak. Rather in such cases each might only have *partial* moral responsibility (jointly with the others), or perhaps a *share* in the moral responsibility, for the realization of the collective end.

1.5 Fingerprinting: Key Ethical Issues

Fingerprint identification techniques conveniently exemplify many of the ethical issues raised by biometric identification methods discussed in this book and, in particular, DNA, facial recognition technology and biometric databases. That said, for the most part fingerprint identification techniques raise these issues in a less acute form. This is because fingerprint identification (including, therefore, databases of fingerprints) is arguably less invasive of privacy and, therefore, less invasive of autonomy than DNA and facial recognition technology. The inherited nature of DNA means there are potentially implications beyond the identification of single individuals, and further, DNA can also potentially be analysed to obtain health and other information; while facial images can be more readily obtained than fingerprints, such as through CCTV, or from online searches.

Here it is important to distinguish the process by which fingerprints (or other biometric data) might be obtained and the right to control one's biometric data. The process of acquiring fingerprints might need to be coercive, e.g. in relation to an offender who resists providing his fingerprints to police, though they may also be freely given to a technology company or financial institution in order to utilise them as a security feature of a device or account. However, it does not follow from this that the possession of one's fingerprints is more invasive than, for instance, the possession of one's DNA.

On the other hand, from a law enforcement and security perspective, arguably fingerprint identification techniques (and databases of fingerprints) are less powerful than DNA and facial recognition technology (and their respective databases), although as discussed above, different biometrics may be more or less relevant or useful depending on the context, or used in unison to provide greater confidence in an identification. DNA traces are more ubiquitous and more reliable than fingerprints. Facial images (once made) can be more effectively used for identification purposes than fingerprints since identification via fingerprints relies essentially on databases of fingerprints whereas facial images, in addition to being stored in databases (e.g. of drivers' licenses), are communicable to the population at large (e.g. via TV news) and searchable on social and other media. Moreover, facial recognition technology provides a powerful tracking mechanism (e.g. via networks of CCTV cameras) (Smith et al., 2018).

Biometric databases, whether of fingerprints, DNA or facial images, are an increasingly important law enforcement and national security tool for intelligence, investigative and evidential purposes but, as already mentioned, they raise ethical issues. However, it is the interlinking of biometric databases with one another and with non-biometric databases (e.g. health and financial databases) that provides the most powerful law enforcement and national security tool but which also raises the most profound ethical concerns. Here the spectre of an authoritarian 'big brother' state looms, of which contemporary China is increasingly being seen as an exemplar.

What are the ethical or moral (we use these terms interchangeably) issues raised by biometric technologies, including both moral benefits as well as moral costs? The most obvious are: (1) privacy and, relatedly confidentiality and individual autonomy; (2) security, e.g. against terrorism and organized crime; (3) power imbalances, e.g. between the government and the citizens; (4) democratic accountability. Additional ethical or moral issues that are perhaps less obvious include the moral right to ownership of one's genetic data, the right not to self-incriminate, and the collective moral responsibility on the part of members of the citizenry to combat crime (or, at least, to assist law enforcement to do so). Three overarching moral issues are, firstly, as we have just seen collective responsibility for the collective good of security and, therefore, to establish, for instance, fingerprint databases; secondly, the liberal-democratic state and the preservation of its constitutive values and; thirdly (and, relatedly), the so-called dual use dilemma in relation to new and emerging technology (in this instance, biometrics). Dual use dilemmas arise in relation to new and emerging technologies as a result of the potential conflict between, on the one hand, the extraordinary actual or potential benefits they confer e.g. in crime reduction and, on the other hand, the actual and potential harms they cause, e.g. infringements, if not violations, of moral rights to privacy and autonomy.

Considered on its own, the use of fingerprint technology by law enforcement and national security agencies seems relatively morally unproblematic, at least under certain conditions, e.g. if fingerprint collection is restricted to crime scenes and fingerprint databases consist only of the fingerprints of those convicted of crimes or reasonably suspected of crimes. In addition, epistemic concerns need to be addressed, e.g. chain of custody of evidence, prints are of good quality and judgements thereof that are used in criminal trials are made and scrutinised by appropriately qualified and experienced experts, and even then considered in the context of other relevant evidence.

However, fingerprint technology is now used by many countries at national borders and, therefore, to reliably identify travelers, irrespective of whether they have criminal convictions or are suspected of any crime (they are now widely used as a security feature in a broad range of civilian contexts). Such use might be justified in terms of border protection and, therefore, national security, albeit on the condition that it not be used for other purposes and that it be subject to stringent accountability mechanisms. The argument here might have recourse to the collective good of security (Miller, 2010 Ch. 2) to which each traveler ought to be prepared to make a contribution by providing fingerprint. They ought to make a contribution because they enjoy the collective good (the security) that is provided by the database of fingerprints. To enjoy this security and yet refuse to allow one's fingerprints at the border would be to unfairly free-ride. Of course, free-riding might be justified if the costs borne were greater by some individuals or were violations of rights and, specifically, in the case of fingerprints, the right to privacy and/or autonomy. On the other hand, an individual can sometimes be expected to bear a minor cost for the sake of the greater good, even if the individual does not personally benefit from that good (Miller, 2010, pp. 337–8).

As mentioned above, and will become clearer in later chapters, fingerprint technology may be considered less invasive than, for example, facial recognition technology. One may not as easily claim ownership of one's fingerprints in the sense of the impressions one's fingers leave on certain surfaces in comparison with a claim that they own or, at least, should have some rights with respect to, photos taken of one's face. Perhaps because although one's face is more visually accessible to others than the patterns on the skin of one's fingers, one's face is constitutive of one's personal identify in a more profound sense than patterns on the skin of one's fingers. The latter may enable a person to be uniquely identified but they do not significantly contribute to a person being who they are.

Given fingerprint technology is an effective tool in law enforcement and in the service of national security, including for purposes of border protection, and given there is no less invasive technology available and fingerprint technology is not particularly invasive, it seems that the argument from the collective moral good of security and, therefore, the existence of a collective moral responsibility to establish fingerprint databases and use fingerprint technology, and the concomitant moral obligation not to free-ride, is persuasive. However, it is important to note that this argument does not demonstrate that *universal* fingerprint databases ought to be established. For one might be under a moral obligation to provide one's fingerprint for exculpatory purposes in relation to a specific crime only; in which case storage in a universal database (as opposed to a database of the fingerprints of those who have committed a crime or are currently suspected of doing so). Naturally, there are other security purposes, e.g. border control, that would justify a database of travelers but again this is short of a universal database and might require a warrant if it were to be accessed for other purposes.

A further set of related questions arise as to whether the use of fingerprint technology can be morally justified outside criminal justice or national security contexts, e.g. in the private sector. Presumably, fingerprint technology could be justified in circumstances in which those whose fingerprints were being used had given their consent in the following strong sense of consent. Here it is important to note that *strong* consent (which may extend further than the legal requirements of consent or than the requirements of weaker non-legal definitions) to an action necessitates that: (i) the agent of the action is a rational adult who intentionally performs the action; (ii) the agent is reasonably well-informed regarding the action; (iii) the action is optional in the sense that the agent can choose not to perform it (as might not be the case if the agent is coerced); (iv) the agent in choosing the action is not being *unjustly* deprived of some *essential* good or service to which the agent has a *moral right*, as might be the case if the agent could not have a bank account or use a computer unless the agent consented (in some weaker sense) to the use of fingerprint technology to access the account or to use the computer. However, the use of fingerprint technology might be morally justified in the private sector, as in the public sector, if the moral weight of the collective good which it served overrode the individual rights infringed and, in particular, if the collective good of security overrode the privacy rights infringed. Consider, for example, the health records held in a private sector database which might be vulnerable to hacking and, therefore, ransomware attacks unless stringent security measures were in place, including the use of the biometric identification technique of fingerprinting. On the other hand, there would need to be assurances that the database of fingerprints was itself secure. For if not its value as a protective measure in relation to health records may well be greatly reduced.

1.6 Conclusion

The development of biometric identification began with a classification system for fingerprints in the mid-nineteenth century and was quickly applied to legal contexts, such as criminal investigation. Today, along with DNA identification and facial recognition, biometric applications are not only used in law enforcement, but have expanded to other areas of society, such as security access in personal devices such as smartphones. Applied ethics plays a key role in determining and justifying how these expanding uses should be regulated by law, providing systematic analysis of the associated values, such as balancing the moral weight to be given to privacy against the benefits delivered by biometric databases in the specific contexts. We argue that the use of biometric technology for certain limited purposes and contexts are a matter of collective moral responsibility and illustrated this using the actors involved in using fingerprint evidence in a criminal investigation. However, we argued that this collective moral responsibility does not extend to the creation of universal fingerprint databases or the accessing of a database justifiably established for one purpose, (e.g. a database of the fingerprints of holders of a bank account), being accessed for another purpose (e.g. by law enforcement officers) without an adequate justification (and in compliance with appropriate legal accountability measures, such as a judicial warrant). We note that fingerprint identification technology is likely to be less morally problematic than other biometrics, such as facial recognition and DNA identification, and that their use, in public or private sector settings can be justified in circumstances in which more invasive technologies are not. Relevant factors in this assessment include the existence of strong consent (as defined above), and where the moral weight of the collective good of security override the privacy rights infringed.

References

Alexandra, A., & Miller, S. (2009a). *Ethics in practice: Moral theory and the professions.* UNSW Press.
Alexandra, A., & Miller, S. (2009b). Ethical theory, 'Common Morality' and professional obligations. *Theoretical Medicine and Bioethics, 30*(1), 69–80.

Allen, R., Sankar, P., & Prabhakar, S. (2005). Fingerprint identification technology. In J. L. Wayman, A. K. Jain, D. Maltoni, & D. Maio (Eds.), *Biometric systems: Technology, design and performance evaluation* (pp. 22–61). Springer.

Ashbourn, J. (2000). *Biometrics: Advanced identity verification*. Springer.

Australian Criminal Intelligence Commission (ACIC). (2019). *Annual report 2018–2019*. Australian Government.

Australian Criminal Intelligence Commission (ACIC). (2020). *Biometric and forensic services*. https://www.acic.gov.au/services/biometric-and-forensic-services

Canadian Government. (2017). *International use of biometrics*. http://www.cic.gc.ca/english/department/biometrics-international.asp

Edmond, G. (2015). Forensic science evidence and the conditions for rational (jury) evaluation. *Melbourne University Law Review, 39*, 77–121.

Federal Bureau of Investigation (FBI). (2017). *Integrated automated fingerprint identification system*. http://www.fbi.gov/about-us/cjis/fingerprints_biometrics/iafis/iafis

Gert, B. (2004). *Common Morality*. Oxford University Press.

Holland. P., & Tham T. (2020, April). Workplace biometrics: Protecting employee privacy one fingerprint at a time. *Economic and Industrial Democracy*, 1–15.

Hopkins, R. (1999). An introduction to biometrics and large scale civilian identification. *International Review of Law, Computers and Technology., 13*, 337–363.

Jain, A., Ross, A., & Pankanti, S. (2006). Biometrics: A tool for information security. *IEEE Transactions on Information Forensics and Security, 1*(2), 125–143.

Lodinová, A. (2016). Application of biometrics as a means of refugee registration: Focusing on UNHCR's strategy. *Development, Environment and Foresight, 2*(2), 91.

Miller, S. (1992). Joint action. *Philosophical Papers, XXI*(3), 275–299.

Miller, S. (1995). Intentions, ends and joint action. *Philosophical Papers, XXIV*(1), 51–67.

Miller, S. (2001a). *Social action: A teleological account*. Cambridge University Press.

Miller, S. (2001b). Collective responsibility and omissions. *Business and Professional Ethics, 20*(1), 5–24.

Miller, S. (2006). Collective moral responsibility: An individualist account. *Midwest Studies in Philosophy, XXX*, 176–193.

Miller, S. (2010). *The moral foundations of social institutions: A philosophical study*. Cambridge University Press.

Miller, S. (2014). Police detectives, criminal investigations and collective responsibility. *Criminal Justice Ethics, 33*(1), 21–39.

Miller, S. (2015). Joint epistemic action and collective responsibility. *Social Epistemology, 29*(3), 280–302.

Miller, S. (2018). Joint epistemic action: Some applications. *Journal of Applied Philosophy, 35*(2), 300–318.

Miller, S., & Gordon, I. (2014). *Investigative ethics: Ethics for police detectives and criminal investigators*. Wiley-Blackwell.

Milne, R. (2013). *Forensic intelligence*. CRC Press.

Moses, K., Higgins, P., McCabe, M., Probhakar, S., & Swann, S. (2010). Automated fingerprint identification system. In *Fingerprint Sourcebook*. National Institute of Justice.

Northrop Grumman. (2017). *IDENT1 automated fingerprint system, United Kingdom*. http://www.homelandsecurity-technology.com/projects/ident1-automated-fingerprint-system-northrop-grumman-uk/

Saferstein, R. (2015). *Criminalistics: An introduction to forensic science*. Pearson Education.

Simonetti, J., Rowhani-Rahbar, A., & Rivara, F. (2017). The road ahead for personalized firearms. *JAMA Internal Medicine., 177*(1), 9–10.

Smith, M. (2016). *DNA evidence in the Australian legal system*. Lexis Nexis.

Smith, M., Mann, M., & Urbas, G. (2018). *Biometrics, crime and security*. Routledge.

Van den Hoven, J., Miller, S., & Pogge, T. (2017). *Designing-in-ethics*. Cambridge University Press.

Open Access This chapter is licensed under the terms of the Creative Commons Attribution 4.0 International License (http://creativecommons.org/licenses/by/4.0/), which permits use, sharing, adaptation, distribution and reproduction in any medium or format, as long as you give appropriate credit to the original author(s) and the source, provide a link to the Creative Commons license and indicate if changes were made.

The images or other third party material in this chapter are included in the chapter's Creative Commons license, unless indicated otherwise in a credit line to the material. If material is not included in the chapter's Creative Commons license and your intended use is not permitted by statutory regulation or exceeds the permitted use, you will need to obtain permission directly from the copyright holder.

Chapter 2
Facial Recognition and Privacy Rights

Abstract Biometric facial recognition is one of the most rapidly developing methods of biometric identification, with expanding applications across law enforcement, government and the private sector. Its capacity for integration with other technologies, such as closed circuit television (CCTV) and social media, differentiate it from DNA and fingerprint biometric identification. This chapter commences with a discussion of the technique of facial recognition and applications in identity verification, public surveillance, and the identification of unknown suspects. Its relative advantages and disadvantages, and the development of facial recognition around the world is explored. The discussion then examines how facial recognition databases developed from existing databases, such as driver's licence photographs, can be integrated with CCTV systems, and most recently, with photographs from social media and the internet. The chapter then considers relevant ethical principles, including privacy, autonomy, security and public safety, and the implications for law and regulation in relation to facial recognition.

Keywords Biometric identification · Biometric database · Facial recognition · Closed circuit television (CCTV) · Social media · Privacy · Security

2.1 Facial Recognition

The historical precursor to facial recognition technology is the traditional identification sketch, made on the basis of eyewitness accounts of suspects in criminal investigations (Valentine & Davis, 2015). This was followed by the examination of photographic or CCTV images by an expert, such as an anatomist, when these technologies became available – police and prosecutors are obviously seeking to prove that a specific defendant is depicted in the images and therefore implicated in a crime. This process can involve either quantitative mapping, incorporating the

---

Note: Some parts of this article were previously published in
Smith, M., & Miller, S. (2021). The ethical application of biometric facial recognition technology.
AI & Society. https://doi.org/10.1007/s00146-021-01199-9.

© The Author(s) 2021
M. Smith, S. Miller, *Biometric Identification, Law and Ethics*, SpringerBriefs in Ethics, https://doi.org/10.1007/978-3-030-90256-8_2

comparison of facial feature measurements; or a qualitative examination of the similarities between facial features (Edmond et al., 2009).

Contemporary biometric facial recognition is a digitalised extension of facial mapping, utilising an algorithm to undertake the comparison. In a similar process to that described in fingerprint identification, it is a digital comparison of the arrangement of facial features. The process commences with a digital photograph being taken, and the face scaled and aligned to establish a baseline position. The facial features are then quantified to create a contour map of the position of individual facial features that is converted into a digital template (Ricanek, 2014). In the matching process, pairs of digital templates are compared, and a numerical score derived, representing a probabilistic measure that they are of the same person. System developers establish the threshold of similarity for a match, taking into account a degree of tolerance for false positives and negatives; with scope for a human to make a final determination on a match if necessary (Introna & Nissenbaum, 2010).

The process of verification is undertaken through one-to-one matching: the live comparison of a face with a digital template stored in an identity document, such as a person presenting a passport at border control. In contrast, identification occurs through one-to-many searching: databases of images or CCTV footage are searched in an attempt to establish a match with a photograph of an unknown person. These applications have been respectively described as 'targeted and public' in the case of verification to confirm identity; and 'generalised and invisible' in the case of surveillance in the form of one-to-many searching to identify a suspect (Garvie et al., 2016, p. 2). As will be discussed further shortly, facial recognition can be used to identify people in public places in real time from CCTV footage, or to identify suspects drawing upon the billions of social media images on the internet (Mann & Smith, 2017; Hill, 2020). Facial recognition technology significantly enhances government surveillance capabilities, and in contrast with DNA identification, for example, it can be conducted from a distance without consent.

However, in spite of these advantages over other biometrics, it also has limitations. Facial recognition does not have the same degree of accuracy as fingerprint or DNA identification, and the frequency that facial features occur in the general population is unknown (Smith, et al., 2018). The technique is limited by the quality of images, the similarity of the environment where images were taken, the age of images, the similarity of cameras used, and the size of the cohort of database images for comparison (Introna & Nissenbaum, 2010). Moreover, changes in an individual's face over time, could result in false positive or negative matches. Relevant factors include: aging, cosmetic surgery, make up, weight gain or loss, hair length, glasses, masks and head wear such as scarves (Samuels, 2017). These issues are exacerbated when using facial recognition technology in relation to non-stationary subjects in uncontrolled conditions, such as real-time CCTV footage. In these circumstances, the accuracy of facial recognition can be impacted by magnification, field of view, orientation and light conditions (Grother et al., 2017).

There have been significant applications and legal developments in relation to biometric facial recognition in Australia, the United States and the United Kingdom over the past 20 years. The technology was integrated into international border control security systems following the 9/11 terrorist attacks on the United States in 2001, and the International Civil Aviation Organisation (ICAO) nominated facial recognition as the global standard for interoperable biometric passports in the early 2000s (Clarke, 2011). Most international airports now have SmartGate technology that automatically scans and compares traveller's faces with biometric identifiers stored within electronic passports (Colley, 2016).

2.1.1 Databases

In contrast with fingerprint or DNA identification databases, governments do not need to obtain facial templates suitable for a facial recognition database specifically for that purpose. Extensive existing repositories (driver licence and passport photographs) have already been created that are suitable for integration with facial recognition technology. Suspect and convicted offender 'mug shot' photograph records are also available, and since 2020, the hundreds of billions of high quality photographs of individuals that have been uploaded to the internet are another potential resource (Hill, 2020). It is clear that facial recognition technology represents a powerful identification tool that has been quickly adopted and integrated with existing law enforcement data systems.

Since 2017, the potential introduction of a national facial biometric matching capability in Australia has been debated, and developments in this jurisdiction provide a useful case study. Legislation has been proposed that would allow a range of federal agencies to share and search facial templates from drivers' licences, passports and other sources. Participating agencies include the Department of Foreign Affairs and Trade, the Department of Home Affairs, the Australian Federal Police, and the Australian Security Intelligence Organisation. Approximately half of the Australian general population hold biometric passports, and the vast majority of the adult population hold drivers licences, meaning that the searching capability of the proposed national database would be approximately 20 million citizens, 80% of the population (Mann & Smith, 2017).

These developments can be traced back to the introduction of biometric passports in the early 2000s. At the state level, incremental legal development has been identified as far back as 2009, when biometric facial recognition compatibility was introduced in New South Wales (NSW) by amending the regulations governing drivers' licences, allowing these images to be searched with biometric systems.[1] In 2015, further regulations were introduced, permitting the release of biometric drivers licence photographs to state police and federal law enforcement and security agencies. Under this change, photographs could be released for biometric matching

---

[1] The regulations were made pursuant to the *Road Transport (Driver Licensing) Act 1998* (NSW), which was later repealed by Schedule 1 of the *Road Transport Legislation (Repeal and Amendment) Act 2013* (NSW).

in relation to the investigation of 'relevant criminal activity', or a 'terrorist act', and this could take place without a warrant or knowledge of the individuals concerned. Because this was effected through a change to regulations, rather than legislation, it occurred without public debate of the capabilities being implemented.

At the federal level in 2015, the government sought to establish a national facial recognition system with the capacity to verify identity through one-to-one matching of documents; and undertake one-to-many searching of databases. In additional to state and territory drivers licence photographs, it also incorporated passport images. In a similar approach to the NSW amendments, the federal government sought to implement this system by changing Commonwealth regulations. The lack of transparency of this approach was criticised, and subsequently legislation was introduced in the national parliament to provide the legal authority for the database (Mann & Smith, 2017).

The legislation authorised the Department of Home Affairs to develop, operate and maintain: an 'interoperability hub' through which participating agencies and organisations can request and transmit biometric facial images and information contained in government identity documents such as driver licenses, but not actually store the images on a federal database. The legislation also proposed that the private sector have limited access to the database to verify the identity of individuals they undertake business with, an aspect that was flagged as creating regulatory complexities and further risks (Mann & Smith, 2017). The Identity-matching Services Bill 2019 and Australian Passports Amendment (Identity-matching Services) Bill 2019 were debated in parliament but not enacted into law, following some critical recommendations of an inquiry by the Parliamentary Joint Committee on Intelligence and Security. The Joint Committee determined that there was insufficient oversight included in the legislation for a system with such significant capabilities, questioning who would be authorised to access the database and under what circumstances, access to the system based on warrants, and a threshold for the seriousness of offences that could be investigated using the system (Petrie, 2019).

2.1.2 CCTV Integration

In the United Kingdom, the Police National Computer (PNC) contains photographs that can be integrated with facial recognition technology, along with other biometrics and intelligence data. It has been reported that the size of this holding is approximately 18 million photographs; however, as with the other jurisdictions discussed, driver's license and passport holdings are a relevant purpose (Hopkins & Morris, 2015). The United Kingdom has been a leader in CCTV integration of facial recognition technology, referred to as Smart CCTV. This provides the capacity to undertake real time surveillance, identification, and tracking of individuals in public places, including the potential identification of individuals in crowds, such as a terrorist suspect at a sports event or a thief in a shopping center. An early example of the use of this technology to receive attention was at the 2017 Champions League football final in Cardiff, where attendees were compared with a database of persons of interest (Owen, 2017). Facial recognition technology is being used by police in a range of contexts, including in conjunction with cameras fitted to vehicles, body worn cameras, drones and robots: and any other available forms of live video surveillance (Garvie et al., 2016).

In 2019, the High Court of England and Wales considered the issue of biometric facial recognition being used by police in suspect identification (the *Bridges* case).[2] AFR Locate[3] was used by South Wales Police (SWP) to integrate biometric facial recognition technology with live images acquired via a camera attached to a mobile police van, and comparing the images with those listed on a watch list. Mr Bridges claimed that SWP had processed his image using AFR Locate, and that he was not on any watch list, arguing that this unjustifiably breached his rights under Article 8 of the European Convention on Human Rights (ECHR): 'the right to respect for his private and family life, his home and his correspondence'. Further, he argued that the actions of SWP were not 'necessary in a democratic society' for the 'relevant purposes of public safety and crime prevention'.[4]

In 2019, the High Court of England and Wales accepted that the use of AFR Locate interfered with Mr Bridges' privacy rights, but ruled that this was outweighed by the powers of the police to prevent and detect crime. Interestingly, the Court distinguished biometric facial recognition from other police activities that require a warrant because they considered facial recognition technology not to be invasive:

> A warrant is required to allow the police to enter someone's private property since otherwise, the act of entering someone's private property without permission would amount to a trespass. Equally, since the act of taking fingerprints generally requires the cooperation of, or use of force on, the subject and would otherwise amount to an assault, statutory powers were enacted to enable the police to take fingerprints. Both involve physically intrusive acts. By contrast, the use of AFR Locate to obtain biometric information is very different. No physical entry, contact or force is necessary when using AFR Locate to obtain biometric data. It simply involves taking a photograph of someone's face and the use of algorithms to attempt to match it with photographic images of faces on a watchlist. The method is no more intrusive than the use of CCTV in the streets.[5]

---

[2] *R (on the application of Edward Bridges) v The Chief Constable of South Wales* [2019] EWHC 2341.

[3] AFR (Automated Facial Recognition).

[4] European Convention on Human Rights Article 8 – Right to respect for private and family life

1. Everyone has the right to respect for his private and family life, his home and his correspondence.
2. There shall be no interference by a public authority with the exercise of this right except such as is in accordance with the law and is necessary in a democratic society in the interests of national security, public safety or the economic well-being of the country, for the prevention of disorder or crime, for the protection of health or morals, or for the protection of the rights and freedoms of others.

[5] [2019] EWHC 2341, 75.

A further issue raised by Mr Bridges was that the AFR Locate technology was new and not regulated by any specific legislation. However, the Court found that this did not preclude its use either:

> In our view, there is a clear and sufficient legal framework governing whether, when and how AFR Locate may be used. What is important is to focus on the substance of the actions that use of AFR Locate entails, not simply that it involves a first-time deployment by SWP of an emerging technology. The fact that a technology is new does not mean that it is outside the scope of existing regulation, or that it is always necessary to create a bespoke legal framework for it.[6]

This decision was appealed to the England and Wales Court of Appeal in 2020,[7] which reversed the 2019 decision, finding that the live automated facial recognition technology used by the South Wales Police Force was unlawful under Article 8 of the ECHR. The Court stated:

> The fundamental deficiencies, as we see it, in the legal framework currently in place relate to two areas of concern. The first is what was called the "who question" at the hearing before us. The second is the "where question". In relation to both of those questions too much discretion is currently left to individual police officers. It is not clear who can be placed on the watchlist nor is it clear that there are any criteria for determining where AFR can be deployed.[8]

A longstanding regulatory development in the United Kingdom is the independent statutory commissioner, established to oversee and respond to concerns relating to consent, retention and use of biometric information by law enforcement agencies in the United Kingdom. The Commissioner for the Retention and Use of Biometric Material[9] seeks to improve the regulation of biometric information and provide a degree of protection from disproportionate law enforcement action.[10] While the Commissioner's powers only currently extend to DNA or fingerprints (OBC, 2020); the House of Commons Science and Technology Committee has recommended that these statutory responsibilities 'be extended to cover, at a minimum, the police use and retention of facial images' (HCSTC, 2015), which may be an impending development after the decision in *Bridges*.

---

[6] [2019] EWHC 2341, 84.

[7] *R (on the application of Bridges) v Chief Constable of South Wales Police* (2020) EWCA Civ 1058.

[8] Ibid, 91.

[9] The UK Biometrics Commissioner was established under the *Protection of Freedoms Act 2012* (UK) in response to the judgement in the *S and Marper v United Kingdom* [2008] ECHR 1581 case in the European Court of Human Rights in 2008.

[10] *Protection of Freedoms Act 2012* (UK) c 9, s 20.

2.1.3 Social Media Integration

The use of facial recognition technology by social media companies headquartered in the United States, followed the development of government databases since 2000, which will initially be briefly considered. The federal facial recognition database is known as the Next Generation Identification (NGI) system. Operated by the Federal Bureau of Investigation, it integrates facial templates with biometrics and other forms of intelligence and has the capacity to search state driver's license databases and other vast repositories. The FBI's facial-recognition capability facilitates 'access to local, state and federal databases containing more than 641 million face photos' (Harwell, 2019). These databases include the US Visitor and Immigrant Status Indicator Technology (US-VISIT) program which collects biometrics from all non-citizens entering the US. Other agencies that may have access to facial recognition searching in the United States include Customs and Border Protection, Coast Guard, Citizenship and Immigration Services, the Department of State, Department of Defence, and Department of Justice, as well as the law enforcement and intelligence communities. On a case-by-case basis, the United States government provides access to facial image repositories for partner countries such as Australia, Canada, New Zealand, and the United Kingdom (USDHS, 2015). In recent years, access to state drivers license databases for facial recognition searching without legislative backing at the state or federal level, or consent of the individuals concerned, has been controversial and debated in congress – further law reform is likely (Harwell, 2019).

The private sector in the United States, in collaboration with law enforcement agencies, have been pioneering another significant application of facial recognition – the analysis of internet-based images from social media sites such as Facebook, Twitter, Instagram, LinkedIn, and Google. There has been a massive expansion in the number of images available on the Internet in recent years: in 2012, Facebook alone held over 100 billion photos in its database, by 2020 that number more than doubled to 250 billion (Hill, 2020).

Facebook uses facial recognition technology to 'tag' photographs with users' names, linking images to individuals' pages and also allowing individuals to be tagged irrespective of whether they have a Facebook page. The Hamburg Commissioner of Data Protection launched a legal challenge to Facebook's facial recognition tagging feature under German data protection and privacy laws; and in 2012, the Irish Data Protection Commissioner audited Facebook's use of face recognition that led to Facebook disabling this feature in the Europe, and deleting stored biometric information previously collected (Mann & Smith, 2017). In 2018, it returned as an opt-in feature in Europe, but remains an opt-out feature in other regions of the world (Kelion, 2018).

In 2020, it became public that police in the United States were using a facial recognition algorithm, developed by the technology company Clearview AI, to search images on the internet in an attempt to identify suspects in investigations (Hill, 2020). It was also reported that police in other countries around the world, such as Australia, were also using Clearview AI's algorithm (Bogle, 2020). Compared with national databases of passport and drivers' licence images, or scanning CCTV footage for suspects; the Clearview AI development, with a capacity to search billions of facial images on the internet in minutes, represents a massive advancement. Significantly, it was also reported that Clearview AI was not only providing facial recognition software to law enforcement agencies, but also private companies, such as Walmart, AT&T, the NBA, Bank of America and Best Buy, for private security purposes.[11]

Legal action against Clearview AI has since commenced. Immediately after the use of the company's services was publicised, the State of New Jersey and social media companies, including Twitter and Facebook, sent cease-and-desist letters asserting that the company had unlawfully obtained users' images (BBC, 2020). A number of class actions were launched. One of these, commenced against Clearview AI by the law firm Haeggquist & Eck, LLP, alleged that Clearview AI violated the provisions of a number of statutes, including the *California Consumer Privacy Act of 2018* (CCPA), raising several issues on behalf of the plaintiffs:

- The individuals did not consent to the use or redistribution of photographs, biometric information and identifiers;
- Clearview AI 'scraped' the images from internet-based websites, in violation of several of the websites' terms of use;
- Clearview AI applied facial recognition software in violation of the CCPA and BIPA;
- Clearview AI sold access to photographs, biometric information and identifiers to third-party entities for commercial gain without consent; and
- Damages were suffered in terms of the diminution in value of individuals' biometric information, and identifiers and placed them at risk of privacy violation.[12]

West (2021) describes the role of social media posts in the investigation of the violence that occurred at the United States Capitol in January 2021, following the outcome of the presidential election. Many rioters posted incriminating images of themselves in and around the Capitol Building, including committing crimes such as trespass and vandalism. The Federal Bureau of Investigation was able to quickly identify many of those responsible, in some cases within hours of the offences being committed, with very strong evidence to provide to prosecutors and obtain a conviction. The role of social media in both enabling the event and in holding those responsible accountable is interesting to observe.

These recent developments add further complexity to the legal and ethical issues associated with biometric facial recognition– the reported use of the technology by

---

[11] Statement of Claim, *State of Vermont v Clearview AI*, Vermont Superior Court, 10 March 2020, 8.

[12] Haeggquist & Eck, LLP, *Sean Burke and James Pomerene, Individually and on Behalf of All Others Similarly Situated, Plaintiffs v. Clearview AI, Inc., a Delaware Corporation*; *Hoan Ton-That, an Individual*; *Richard Schwartz, an Individual*; *and Does 1 through 10, inclusive, Defendants*, United States District Court Southern District of California. Class Action Complaint Demand for Jury Trial. Case Number: 20CV0370 BAS MSB, 5–8.

private sector companies such as banks and retailers is more concerning than use by law enforcement. While legal constraints associated with Clearview AI's use of images held by social media companies may ultimately threaten its feasibility and ability to provide its services to the private sector; this is less likely to be an issue for a law enforcement agency, and further regulation and guidance through legislative reform is needed.

2.2 Ethical Principles

The expanding use of biometric facial recognition raises a number of pressing ethical concerns for liberal democracies. The concerns relate especially to the potential conflicts between security, on the one hand, and individual privacy and autonomy, and democratic accountability, on the other. Security and community safety are fundamental values in liberal democracies, as in other polities, including many authoritarian ones. However, liberal democracies are also committed to individual privacy and autonomy, democracy, and therefore, democratic accountability. Accordingly, the latter fundamental ethical principles must continue to be valued in a liberal democracies such as Australia, the United Kingdom and the United States, notwithstanding the benefits to security and community safety that biometric facial recognition can provide (Miller & Bossomaier, 2021). While debates will continue between proponents of security, on the one hand, and defenders of privacy, on the other, there is often a lack of clarity in relation to the values or principles allegedly in conflict.

2.2.1 Privacy

The notion of privacy has proven difficult to adequately explicate (Benn, 1988; Miller, 1997; Etzioni, 1999; Miller & Weckert, 2000; Nagel, 2002; Kleinig et al., 2011). Nevertheless, there are a number of general points that can be made (Benn, 1988; Miller, 1997; Nagel, 2002; Macnish, 2017; Henschke, 2017). First, privacy is a right that people have in relation to other persons, the state and organisations with respect to: (a) the possession of information (including facial images) about themselves by other persons and by organisations, e.g. personal information and images stored in biometric databases, or; (b) the observation/perceiving of themselves – including of their movements, relationships and so on – by other persons, e.g. via surveillance systems including tracking systems that rely on biometric facial images. Biometric facial recognition is obviously implicated in both informational and observational concerns.

Second, the right to privacy is closely related to the more fundamental moral value of autonomy (Benn, 1988; Miller, 1997; Nagel, 2002). Roughly speaking, the notion of privacy delimits an informational and observational 'space' i.e. the private sphere. However, the right to autonomy consists of a right to decide what to think and do and, of relevance here, the right to control the private sphere and, therefore, to decide *who to exclude and who not to exclude* from it. So the right to privacy consists of the right to exclude organisations and other individuals (the right to autonomy) both from personal information and facial images, and from observation and monitoring (the private sphere).

As noted in Chap. 1, the moral right to control some element of the private sphere does not necessarily depend on the difficulty attaching to exercising that right. A person has a moral right that others not trespass on his land, irrespective of whether his land is fenced or he has the means to exclude them. Again, a person has a moral right not to be photographed in her shower, irrespective of whether or not a long range camera is able to take photo of her in the shower in her home from outside her property. The 2019 High Court of England and Wales decision in *Bridges* did not invoke this morally (but perhaps not legally) relevant conceptual distinction. In the 2020 Court of Appeal decision, the Court raised what they termed the 'where question' finding that there appeared to be too much discretion left to individual police officers with respect to where they could deploy the technology, in addition to the question of who it could lawfully be deployed against, in light of Article 8 of the ECHR.

By contrast with the degree of difficulty attaching to exercising one's right, the moral right to control some element of the privacy sphere can depend on the moral weight of that element and, of relevance to facial technology, it's centrality to a person's personal identity (Nagel, 2002 Ch. 1; Henschke, 2017). Evidently, one's face is constitutive of one's personal identity; hence one has a moral right to control images of one's face. Conversely, it might be argued that one's face is necessarily present to others and, therefore, one does not, because one cannot, have a right to control images of it. Certainly, one's face is a central tool of interpersonal expression and communication. However, it does not follow from this that one does not have a right to control images of it. Firstly, we need to distinguish one's face from images of it. Logically, one could have a right to control images of one's face even if one had limited control over who saw one's face in the flesh (so to speak). Secondly, one can in fact exercise considerable control over which interpersonal contexts one participates in and, therefore, who sees one's face. Moreover, one can also exercise control over how one presents one's self in the company of others, e.g. one can choose to conceal or feign emotions by controlling one's facial expressions. Secondly, speaking generally, in these interpersonal context the faces of all those who participate are visible to the others. It is not simply a case of one party doing the looking without being themselves looked at, as is the case with the uncontrolled (by one's-self) dissemination of one's facial image.

Naturally, the right to privacy is not absolute; it can be overridden. Moreover, its precise boundaries are unclear; a person does not have a right not to be observed in a public space but, arguably, has a right not to be photographed in a public space (let alone have an image of their face widely circulated on the internet), albeit this right not to be photographed and have one's image circulated can be overridden under certain circumstances (Miller & Gordon, 2014 Ch. 10; Miller & Blackler, 2016 Ch. 4; Kleinig et al., 2011). For instance, this right might be overridden if the public space in question is under surveillance by CCTV in order to detect and deter crime, and if the resulting images are only made available to police – and then only for the purpose of identifying persons who have committed a crime in that area. What of persons who are present in the public space in question and recorded on CCTV, but who have committed a serious crime, such as terrorism, elsewhere, or at least are suspected of having committed a serious crime[13] elsewhere and are, therefore, on a watch-list? Presumably, it is morally acceptable to utilise CCTV footage to identify these persons as well. If so, then it seems morally acceptable to utilize biometric facial recognition technology to match images of persons recorded on CCTV with those of persons on a watch-list of those who have committed, for instance, terrorist actions, or are suspected of having done so, as the SWP were arguably seeking to do in the *Bridges* case.

Third, a degree of privacy is necessary simply in order for people to pursue their personal projects, whatever those projects might be (Benn, 1988). For one thing, reflection is necessary for planning, and reflection requires a degree of freedom from the distracting intrusions, including intrusive surveillance, of others. For another, knowledge of someone else's plans can lead to those plans being thwarted (e.g. if one's political rivals can track one's movements and interactions then they can come to know one's plans in advance of their implementation), or otherwise compromised, (e.g. if who citizens vote for is not protected by a secret ballot, including a prohibition on cameras in private voting booths, then democracy can be compromised).

We have so far considered the rights of a *single* individual; however, it is important to consider the implications of the infringement, indeed violation, of the privacy and autonomy rights of the whole citizenry by the state (and/or other powerful institutional actors, such as corporations). Such violations on a large scale can lead to a power imbalance between the state and the citizenry and, thereby, undermine liberal democracy itself (Miller & Walsh, 2016). The surveillance system imposed on the Uighurs in China, incorporating biometric facial recognition technology, graphically illustrates the risks attached to large scale violations of privacy and related autonomy rights.

Accordingly, while it is morally acceptable to collect biometric facial images for necessary circumscribed purposes, such as passports for border control purposes and drivers' licences for safety purposes, it is not acceptable to collect them to establish vast surveillance states as China has done, and exploit them to discriminate on the basis of ethnicity. However, images in passports and driving licences are, and arguably ought to be, available for *wider* law enforcement purposes, e.g. to assist in tracking the movements of persons suspected of serious crimes unrelated to border control or safety on the roads. The issue that now arises is the determination of the point on the spectrum at which privacy and security considerations are appropriately balanced.

---

[13] We will define a serious crime as an offence punishable by imprisonment for a term of 3 or more years.

Privacy can reasonably be overridden by security considerations under some circumstances, such as when lives are at risk. After all, the right to life is, in general, a weightier moral right than the right to privacy (Miller & Blackler, 2016 Ch. 4; Miller & Gordon, 2014 Ch. 10; Miller & Walsh, 2016). Thus, utilising facial recognition technology to investigate a serious crime such as a murder or track down a suspected terrorist, if conducted under warrant, is surely ethically justified. On the other hand, intrusive surveillance of a suspected petty thief might not be justified, even assuming it is very effective. Here key principles that need to be invoked are necessity and proportionality (Miller, 2021; Henschke, 2017; Macnish, 2017). Is it necessary to use facial recognition technology or would a less invasive means suffice? And, even if it is necessary, is it proportionate? Evidently, widespread use of facial recognition technology in conjunction with facial recognition technology would be a disproportionate response to a few instances of petty crime. Moreover, given the importance of, so to speak, the aggregate privacy/autonomy of the citizenry, threats to life on a small scale might not be of sufficient weight to justify substantial infringements of privacy/autonomy, e.g. a low level terrorist threat might not justify citizen-wide biometric facial recognition database. Again, the principles of necessity and proportionality are relevant, albeit this time at the macro society-wide level (Miller, 2021). Further, regulation, and associated accountability mechanisms need to be in place to ensure that, for instance, a database of biometric facial images created for a legitimate purpose, e.g. a repository of passport photos, can be accessed by border security and law enforcement officers to enable them to prevent and detect serious crimes, such as murder, but not used to identify protesters at a political rally.

We have argued that privacy rights, including in respect of biometric facial images, are important, in part because of their close relation to autonomy, and although they can be overridden under some circumstances, notably by law enforcement investigations of serious crimes (and given it is effective, necessary and proportionate), there is obviously a point where infringements of privacy rights is excessive and unwarranted. This is obviously the case in relation to privacy rights infringed, indeed violated, simply to generate profits, as in the case of a business model that provides 'free' services in return for personal data without *strong* consent (see Chap. 1), e.g. Facebook's business model. A national biometric facial recognition database for use in relation to serious crimes, and subject to appropriate accountability mechanisms may be acceptable, but utilising billions of images from social media accounts (e.g. in the way that Clearview AI's technology does) to detect and deter minor offences, let alone establishing a surveillance state (e.g. to the extent that has been achieved in China), is clearly unacceptable. Let us now turn directly to security.

2.2.2 Security and Public Safety

Security can refer to, for example, national security (such as harm to public from a terrorist attack), community security (such as in the face of disruptions to law and order) and organisational security (such as breaches of confidentiality and other forms of misconduct and criminality). At other times it is used to refer to personal physical security. Physical security in this sense is security in the face of threats to one's life, freedom or personal property – the latter being goods to which one has a human right. Violations or breaches of physical security obviously include assault and murder (Miller & Gordon, 2014; Miller & Blackler, 2016; Miller & Bossomaier, 2021). Biometric facial recognition systems could assist in multiple ways to enhance security in each of these senses. Thus a biometric facial recognition system could help to prevent fraud by better establishing identity (e.g. identify people using falsified drivers licences) and facial recognition data would be likely to help to investigate serious crimes against persons (e.g. identifying unknown suspects via CCTV footage). However, as mentioned above, its use in relation to less serious crimes, e.g. crimes, such as shoplifting, that are punishable by a prison term of, say, less than three years, evidently would not comply with the principle of proportionality in particular.

Arguably, security should be distinguished from safety, although the two concepts are related and the distinction somewhat blurred (Miller, 2018 Ch. 5 Sec. 5.2). We tend to speak of safety in the context of wildfires, floods, pandemics and the like, in which the harm to be avoided is not intended harm. By contrast, the term 'security' typically implies that the threatened harm is intended. At any rate, it is useful to at least maintain a distinction between intended and unintended harms and, in relation to unintended harms, between foreseen, unforeseen and unforeseeable harms. For instance, someone who is unknowingly carrying the COVID-19 virus because they are asymptomatic, is a danger to others but, nevertheless, might not be culpable (if, for instance, they had taken reasonable measures to avoid being infected, had an intention to test for infection if symptoms were to arise and, if infected, would take all possible measures not to infect others). While biometric facial recognition systems can make an important contribution to security, their utility in relation to safety is less obvious, albeit they could assist in relation to finding missing persons or ensuring unauthorised persons do not unintentionally access dangerous sites (Smith & Miller, 2021).

We have described the expanding use of biometric facial recognition for security and public safety purposes and elaborated on current applications and legal developments in Australia, the United States and the United Kingdom. In light of these applications and developments, we have discussed various ethical principles and concepts, notably privacy and security. We now need to consolidate and specify a number of the more salient ethical problems and principles that arise from the expanding use of biometric facial recognition for security purposes, especially in the context of interlinkage with non-biometric databases, data analytics and artificial intelligence.

First, privacy in relation to personal data, such as facial images, consists in large part in the right to control the access to, and use of, that data. Moreover, given that one's face is a constitutive feature of one's personal identity one has a moral right to exercise control of one's facial images, albeit this moral right is not absolute. Accordingly, this moral right can be overridden by other rights, such as the right to security. However, security consists in large part in individual rights, notably the right to life, as well as to institutional goods, such as law and order. Biometric facial recognition technology gives rise to security concerns, such as the possibility of identity theft by a sophisticated malevolent actor, even as they resolve old privacy and confidentiality concerns, such as by reducing unauthorised access to private information and thereby strengthening privacy protection. In short, the problems in this area cannot be framed in terms of a simple weighing of, let alone trade-off between, individual privacy rights versus the community's interest in security.

Second, the establishment of comprehensive, integrated biometric facial recognition databases and systems by governments (and now the private sector), and the utilisation of this data to identify and track citizens, (e.g. via live CCTV feeds) has the potential to create a power imbalance between governments and citizens, and risks undermining important principles taken to be constitutive of the liberal democratic state, such as privacy.

Third, the security contexts in which their use is to be permitted might become both very wide and continuing, e.g. the counter-terrorism ('emergency') security context becomes the 'war' (without end) against terrorism; which becomes the war (without end) against serious crime; which becomes the 'war' (without end) against crime in general (Miller & Gordon, 2014).

Fourth, the expanding use of biometric facial recognition databases and systems has to be clearly and demonstrably justified in terms of efficiency and effectiveness in the service of *specific* security and/or safety purpose, rather than by general appeals to community security or safety. Relatedly, data, including surveillance data, originally and justifiably gathered for one purpose, e.g. taxation or combating a pandemic, is interlinked with data gathered for another purpose, e.g. crime prevention, without appropriate justification (Miller & Gordon, 2014 Ch. 10; Miller & Blackler, 2016 Ch. 4). The way metadata use has expanded from initially being used by only a few agencies to now being used quite widely by governments in many western countries, is an example of function creep and illustrates the potential problems that might arise with the introduction of biometric facial recognition systems (Mann & Smith, 2017).

Fifth, various general principles taken to be constitutive of liberal democracy are gradually undermined, such as the principle that an individual has a right to freedom from criminal investigation or unreasonable monitoring, absent prior evidence of violation by that individual of its laws. In a liberal democratic state, it is generally accepted that the state has no right to seek evidence of wrongdoing on the part of a particular citizen or to engage in selective monitoring of that citizen, if the actions of the citizen in question have not otherwise reasonably raised suspicion of unlawful behaviour and if the citizen has not had a pattern of unlawful past behaviour that justify monitoring. Moreover, in a liberal democratic state, it is also generally accepted that there is a presumption against the state monitoring the citizenry. This presumption can be overridden for specific purposes but only if the monitoring in question is not disproportionate, is necessary or otherwise adequately justified and kept to a minimum, and is subject to appropriate accountability mechanisms (Miller, 2021). Arguably, the use of CCTV cameras in crime hot-spots could meet these criteria if certain conditions were met, e.g. police access to footage was granted only if a crime was committed or if the movements of a person reasonably suspected of a crime needed to be tracked. However, these various principles are potentially undermined by certain kinds of offender profiling and, specifically, ones in which there is no specific (actual or reasonably suspected) past, imminent or planned crime being investigated (Miller & Gordon, 2014 Ch. 10; Miller & Blackler, 2016 Ch. 4). Biometric facial recognition could be used to facilitate, for instance, a process of offender profiling, risk assessment and subsequent monitoring of people who as a result of fitting these profiles are considered at risk of committing crimes, notwithstanding that the only offences that the individuals in question had committed was to fit these profiles.

Finally, in so far as the use of facial recognition and other biometric identification systems can be justified for specific security (and safety) purposes and, therefore, privacy and other concerns mitigated, it is, nevertheless, imperative that their use be subject to accountability mechanisms to guard against misuse. Citizens should be well informed about biometric facial recognition systems and should have consented to the use of these systems for the specific, justified purposes in question. Their use should be publicly debated, backed by legislation, and their operation subject to judicial review.

2.3 Conclusion

Biometric facial recognition is rapidly becoming very widely used by government and the private sector. It can integrate existing photographs, such as those stored in driver's license registries or posted on the internet and combine with CCTV networks to identify individuals in public spaces. Recent examples, such as the debate about Clearview AI, demonstrate the high value law enforcement agencies place on this form of data, and the concern held by the community in relation to its use for this purpose. We have described the notion of privacy and its relation to autonomy. We have also described the relationship between facial images and personal identity. Biometric facial recognition (in both informational and observational aspects) has the potential to unacceptably compromise privacy, autonomy and personal identity rights; indeed, as mentioned above, it is already being used to do so in Xinjiang in China. Applying the principles of necessity and proportionality, it may be acceptable to use facial recognition in association with CCTV to identify an individual, for example who has, or is suspected of having committed, a serious crime or act of terrorism. However, the use of facial recognition technology in conjunction with CCTV to monitor ordinary citizens (as opposed to monitor a restricted area or to create footage which is only accessed if, for instance, a crime is committed) is not acceptable and should be restricted by legislative protections to prevent this being done on a wide scale and for political purposes, as in China. Moreover, access to CCTV footage should be restricted by law, both in terms of those who are granted access and the purposes for which they are granted access, and access should be subjected to stringent accountability mechanism. Footage should only be destroyed after a reasonable time period other than in exceptional circumstances (e.g. if used in the investigation of a serious crime, and associated court proceedings). Further, the creation of national, and especially universal, facial recognition databases for law enforcement and security purposes from existing repositories of facial images, such as passport or drivers licence databases, is an example of morally unacceptable function creep. More generally, the creation of facial recognition databases needs to be justified in terms of specific, defined, morally acceptable purposes and not, therefore, merely by general appeals to vague notions of community safety, national security, and the like. Moreover, facial recognition databases should not be established without public debate, the consent of the citizenry and supporting legislation and accountability mechanisms.

References

Benn, S. I. (1988). *Theory of Freedom*. Cambridge University Press.
British Broadcasting Corporation (BBC). (2020, January 23). *Twitter demands AI company stops collecting faces*. https://www.bbc.com/news/technology-51220654
Bogle, A. (2020, April 14). Australian federal police officers trialled controversial facial recognition tool Clearview AI. *Australian Broadcasting Corporation News*. https://www.abc.net.au/news/science/2020-04-14/clearview-ai-facial-recognition-tech-australian-federal-police/12146894
Clarke, S. (2011). Balancing privacy and security in the Australian passport system. *Deakin Law Review, 16*(2), 325–360.
Colley, A. (2016, October 21). Govt wants to remove passports from border processing. *ITNews*. https://www.itnews.com.au/news/govt-wants-to-remove-passports-from-border-processing-439785
Edmond, G., Biber, K., Kemp, R., & Porter, G. (2009). Law's looking glass: Expert identification evidence derived from photographic and video images. *Current Issues in Criminal Justice, 20*(3), 337–377.
Etzioni, A. (1999). *Limits of privacy*. Basic Books.
Garvie, C., Bedoya, A., & Frankle, J. (2016). *The perpetual line-up: Unregulated police face recognition in America*. Georgetown Law Centre on Privacy and Technology Report. https://www.perpetuallineup.org/
Grother, P., Quinn, G., & Ngan, M. (2017). *Face in video evaluation (FIVE): Face recognition of non-cooperative subjects*. National Institute of Standards and Technology. https://nvlpubs.nist.gov/nistpubs/ir/2017/NIST.IR.8173.pdf
Harwell, D. (2019, July 8). FBI, ICE find state Driver's license photos are a gold mine for facial-recognition searches. *Washington Post*. https://www.washingtonpost.com/technology/2019/07/07/fbi-ice-find-state-drivers-license-photos-are-gold-mine-facial-recognition-searches/
Henschke, A. (2017). *Ethics in an age of surveillance: Personal information and virtual identities*. Cambridge University Press.
Hill, K. (2020, January 18). The secretive company that might end privacy as we know it. *New York Times*. https://www.nytimes.com/2020/01/18/technology/clearview-privacy-facial-recognition.html

References

Hopkins, N., & Morris, J. (2015, February 3). Innocent people on police photos database. *British Broadcasting Corporation News*. http://www.bbc.com/news/uk-31105678

House of Commons Science and Technology Committee (HCSTC). (2015). *Current and future uses of biometric data and technologies*. United Kingdom Parliament.

Introna, L., & Nissenbaum, H. (2010). Facial recognition technology: A survey of policy and implementation issues. *Lancaster University Working Paper*. http://www.research.lancs.ac.uk/portal/en/publications/facial-recognition-technology-a-survey-of-policy-and-implementation-issues(43367675-c8b9-4644-90f2-86815cc8ea15).html

Kleinig, J., Mameli, P., Miller, S., Salane, D., & Schwartz, A. (2011). *Security and privacy*. ANU Press.

Kelion, L. (2018, April 18). Facebook seeks facial recognition consent in EU and Canada. *British Broadcasting News*. https://www.bbc.com/news/technology-43797128

Macnish, K. (2017). *Surveillance ethics: An introduction*. Routledge.

Mann, M., & Smith, S. (2017). Automated facial recognition technology: Recent developments and approaches to oversight. *UNSW Law Journal, 40*, 121–145.

Miller, S. (1997). Privacy and the internet. *Australian Computer Journal, 29*(1), 12–16.

Miller, S. (2018). *Dual use science and technology, Ethics and weapons of mass destruction*. Springer.

Miller, S. (2021). Rethinking the just intelligence theory of national security intelligence collection and analysis: Principles of discrimination, necessity, proportionality and reciprocity. *Social Epistemology, 35*, 211–231.

Miller, S., & Blackler, J. (2016). *Ethical Issues in Policing*. Routledge.

Miller, S., & Bossomaier, T. (2021). *Ethics and Cybersecurity*. Oxford University Press.

Miller, S., & Gordon, I. (2014). *Investigative ethics: Ethics for police detectives and criminal investigators*. Blackwell.

Miller, S., & Walsh, P. (2016). NSA, Snowden and the ethics and accountability of intelligence gathering. In J. Galliott & J. Reed (Eds.), *Ethics and the future of spying: Technology, intelligence collection and national security* (pp. 193–204). Routledge.

Miller, S., & Weckert, J. (2000). Privacy, the workplace and the internet. *Journal of Business Ethics, 14*(2), 255–265.

Nagel, T. (2002). *Concealment and exposure, and other essays*. Oxford University Press.

Office of the Biometrics Commissioner (OBC). (2020). *About*. https://www.gov.uk/government/organisations/biometrics-commissioner/about

Owen, G. (2017, April 26). British cops will scan every fan's face at the champions league final. *Motherboard*. https://motherboard.vice.com/en_us/article/british-cops-will-scan-every-fans-face-at-the-champions-league-final

Petrie, C. (2019, August 26). *Bills digest No. 21 identity-matching Services Bill 2019 and Australian Passports Amendment (Identity-matching Services) Bill 2019*. Australian Parliamentary Library.

Ricanek, K. (2014, September). Beyond recognition: The promise of biometric analytics. *IEEE Computer Society, 47*, 87–89.

Samuels, G. (2017, January 5). Anti-surveillance clothing unveiled to combat facial recognition technology. *The Independent*. http://www.independent.co.uk/news/science/anti-surveillance-clothing-facial-recognition-technology-hyperface-adam-harvey-berlin-facebook-apple-a7511631.html

Smith, M., Mann, M., & Urbas, G. (2018). *Biometrics, Crime and Security*. Routledge.

Smith, M., & Miller, S. (2021). The ethical application of biometric facial recognition technology. *AI & Society*. https://doi.org/10.1007/s00146-021-01199-9

United States Department of Homeland Security. (2015). *DHS/NPPD/privacy impact assessment: Automated biometric identification system (IDENT)*. https://www.dhs.gov/publication/dhsnppdpia-002-automated-biometric-identification-system-ident

Valentine, T., & Davis, J. (2015). *Forensic facial identification: Theory and practice of identification from eyewitnesses and CCTV*. Blackwell.

West, D. (2021). *Digital fingerprints are identifying Capitol rioters*. The Brookings Institution. https://www.brookings.edu/blog/techtank/2021/01/19/digital-fingerprints-are-identifying-capitol-rioters/

Open Access This chapter is licensed under the terms of the Creative Commons Attribution 4.0 International License (http://creativecommons.org/licenses/by/4.0/), which permits use, sharing, adaptation, distribution and reproduction in any medium or format, as long as you give appropriate credit to the original author(s) and the source, provide a link to the Creative Commons license and indicate if changes were made.

The images or other third party material in this chapter are included in the chapter's Creative Commons license, unless indicated otherwise in a credit line to the material. If material is not included in the chapter's Creative Commons license and your intended use is not permitted by statutory regulation or exceeds the permitted use, you will need to obtain permission directly from the copyright holder.

Chapter 3
DNA Identification, Joint Rights and Collective Responsibility

Abstract DNA identification developed late in the twentieth century and has surpassed fingerprinting as the leading technique for forensic human identification. It differs from the other biometrics discussed in that it is based on principles of biological, rather than physical sciences. Another difference is the time taken to convert a biological sample into a DNA profile; however, this is becoming less significant as technology progresses. DNA is also more accurate and revealing in comparison with other biometrics because it can provide information about a person's physical appearance and health status, as well as link an individual to, and in association with further investigations, identify, their biological relatives. This chapter examines DNA identification in law enforcement, related developments associated with commercial genomic health and ancestry databases, and the potential impact of population wide DNA collection. The ethical analysis considers privacy and autonomy, self-incrimination, joint rights and collective responsibility.

Keywords Biometric identification · DNA identification · DNA profiling · DNA database · Genomics · Forensic genealogy · Privacy · Autonomy · Joint rights

3.1 DNA Identification

DNA can be recovered from biological material, such as skin cells or hair continuously being shed, or from bodily fluids such as blood. DNA obtained at a crime scene or collected via a cheek swab from a suspect is analysed in a laboratory to create a DNA profile. This profile can be compared with one obtained from biological material collected from a suspect or held in a DNA database. DNA identification is vital to modern criminal investigation and continues to be used with success in investigating serious crimes. While it has a strong scientific foundation, controversy

---

Note: Some parts of this article were previously published in
Smith, M., & Miller, S. (2021). A principled approach to cross-sector genomic data access. *Bioethics*. https://doi.org/10.1111/bioe.12919.

has occurred, for example due to contamination or other human errors in collection or laboratory testing, resulting in inaccuracies. DNA is a form of circumstantial evidence and is presented in a criminal trial in the context of a range of other evidence. If there was strong evidence that a defendant could not have been present at a crime scene, for example they were in another location at the time the crime was committed, and their DNA may have been innocently deposited there, it may not incriminate the defendant (Smith, 2016).

Repetitive regions of DNA within the genome, called *short tandem repeats* (STRs), exhibit variation between individuals in terms of the number of repeats present at each site. A DNA profile is created by analysing the number of STRs that occur at specific sites in an individual's genome. The STRs used in DNA identification are present in *non-coding* regions of the human genome: these regions do not code for genes and do not provide any health or other information about the individual aside from their identity. A match between two DNA profiles, such as one from a crime scene sample and one from a suspect sample, provides a strong basis for inferring that the samples are from the same person. An example of a DNA profile is the following gender designation (XY for male; XX for female) and set of paired numbers representing the number of repeats at STR sites on each strand of DNA, for example: 'XY 9,12 18,21 14,16 14,14 15,16 25,28' (Smith, 2016).

DNA identification was first used in a criminal investigation in 1987, when Professor Alec Jeffreys analysed biological samples recovered from two murder victims, and compared these with a sample of a suspect who had confessed to the crime. While it established that the suspect's DNA did not match the sample recovered from the victim, subsequent DNA screening of all the men from three surrounding villages was conducted, and Colin Pitchfork came to attention after coercing another into providing a sample on his behalf. Pitchfork's DNA profile matched one found at the crime scene, leading to his conviction (Jobling & Gill, 2004).

The collection of the biological sample is a critical step in DNA identification. If a sample has been planted at a crime scene, or is otherwise contaminated, the validity of the results can be compromised. It follows that DNA should not be interpreted in isolation of the other evidence in a criminal investigation or trial. The trial of O.J. Simpson in California in the mid-1990s highlighted that despite a firm scientific foundation, if collection procedures are not strictly followed, the value of the evidence can be compromised. In that early case, television footage of the crime scene was used by the defence to demonstrate that investigators had entered the scene without protective clothing, not worn protective gloves, and had dropped swabs on the ground prior to securing them in evidence bags, leading to the evidence being discredited (Smith, 2016).

DNA databases are collections of DNA profiles, indexed into categories, e.g. suspects, convicted offenders, crime scene profiles. A legislative definition of a DNA database is as follows:

> …a database (whether in computerised or other form and however described) containing (a) the following indexes of DNA profiles: a crime scene index, a missing persons index, an unknown deceased persons index, a serious offenders index, a volunteers index, a suspects

index, and information that may be used to identify the person from whose forensic material each DNA profile was derived; (b) a statistical index; and (c) any other index prescribed by the regulations.[1]

Millions of DNA profiles are collected and stored by law enforcement agencies to assist in the investigation of serious crimes, and the size of these holdings continue to grow each year. In 2021, the US National DNA Index System (NDIS) contains over 18.5 million profiles, the UK's National DNA Database (NDNAD) over 6.6 million profiles, and the Australian National Criminal Investigation DNA Database (NCIDD), more than 1.2 million profiles (FBI, 2021; UK Government, 2021; ACIC, 2021). Significantly, the United Kingdom's holding represents 10% of the total population.

There have been proposals to establish population wide DNA databases for law enforcement purposes (also referred to as, universal, in the sense that they could encompass a country's entire population), to improve the investigation of crime. Many would object to a national database of DNA profiles, with individuals (including children) included irrespective of whether they have been convicted of committing a crime, as an affront to their individual privacy and autonomy (Smith, 2018). However, as discussed in Chap. 2, similar databases are being established with other biometrics, such as facial recognition databases, by drawing on repositories of drivers licence and passport images. The following section considers legal developments, including prominent UK cases relating to the retention of DNA profiles from suspects that have not been convicted of a crime– a highly relevant to the potential establishment of population wide forensic databases.

3.2 Legal Issues

In the legal system, legislation and case law governs how DNA evidence can be used in law enforcement investigations and criminal trials. Forensic procedures legislation and evidence law regulates the circumstances in which forensic samples may lawfully be obtained and retained, and when evidence may be admitted at trial.[2] Provisions exist in most jurisdictions to enable evidence that has been obtained improperly, to be admitted if the desirability of admitting the evidence outweighs the undesirability of not doing so, in the context of a particular trial. Therefore, if a court considers evidence to be so important that it would be unjust for it not to be used, it may allow the use of evidence at trial even if investigators obtained it illegally. However, courts will also be concerned that the expert presenting the evidence has the appropriate knowledge, skill, experience, training, or education;

---

[1] Section 23YDAC of the *Crimes Act 1914* (Cth) (Australia).
[2] See, e.g. in the United States, the DNA Fingerprint Act of 2005 allows an arrestee's profile to be uploaded to the federal database at the time of arrest. If the arrestee is not subsequently charged with an offence, the burden lies with the arrestee to file a court order stating that the charges have been dismissed.

whether the evidence is based on reliable scientific principles and methods; and whether it has been tested, subjected to peer review, and is generally accepted in the scientific community.[3]

Whether a law enforcement agency can collect and retain biological samples and create DNA profiles differs by jurisdiction. Generally, criminal procedure legislation in democratic countries around the world requires that there be a reasonable suspicion that a suspect has been involved in a crime before their DNA can be taken; and that they have been convicted an offence, in order for it to be indefinitely retained in a DNA database. In the United States, the Fourth Amendment of the Constitution governs the legitimacy of government intrusion into the lives of private citizens, protecting the 'right of the people to be secure in their persons…against unreasonable searches and seizures'. In order to be considered reasonable, a search needs to be supported by a warrant on the basis of probable cause: the reasonable belief that the individual has committed a crime.

Relevant cases in the United States include *Commonwealth v Cabral*[4] where it was held that there is no violation of the Fourth Amendment when a police investigator, following a rape suspect, observed the suspect spit on the street, and collected the saliva (containing skin cells), prior to establishing a match with the sample recovered from a victim. While the suspect did have a reasonable expectation of privacy in his saliva, when he expectorated and did not retrieve it, he assumed the risk of the public witnessing the act and taking possession of it. In *Cabral*, the court relied on *Commonwealth v Ewing*[5] which found no expectation of privacy in cigarette butts that had been disposed of following a police interview. The more recent Supreme Court case *Maryland v King*[6] also addresses the issue of arrestee DNA. King was arrested on assault charges and his DNA subsequently collected and retained in the state DNA database. Before he was convicted of the assault charge, his DNA profile was found to match a crime scene sample from an unsolved rape case in 2003, and he was convicted of that offence. King argued that the DNA match should have been suppressed because the Maryland DNA collection legislation allowing the database search violated the Fourth Amendment. While the Maryland Court of Appeals found the legislation was unconstitutional, and set aside the rape conviction, the Supreme Court overturned this decision and held that the retention and searching of DNA profiles against databases is a legitimate and constitutionally valid procedure to identify arrestees and determine the level of risk they pose to the community.

A significant case involving the retention of DNA evidence in the United Kingdom and Europe is *R v Marper & S*.[7] This focused on whether the *Criminal*

---

[3] See e.g. in the United States, Federal Rules of Evidence, rule 702; *Daubert v. Merrell Dow Pharmaceuticals, Inc.*, 509 U.S. 579 (1993).
[4] 69 Mass.App.Ct. 68, 2007.
[5] 67 (Mass.App.Ct. 531, 2006).
[6] 569 US 435 (2013).
[7] (2002) EWCA Civ 1275

Justice and Police Act 2001 (UK) contravened Article 8 of the *European Convention on Human Rights* relating to individual privacy. The case related to two individuals (one a 12-year-old child) who were charged with separate offences (the theft of a bike, and a domestic violence that was later dropped). Samples were obtained and DNA profiles created and included in the national DNA database. Following their acquittal, police refused to destroy the DNA profiles. This was appealed to the House of Lords,[8] followed by the European Court of Human Rights, which delivered its decision in December 2008.[9] The Court ruled in favour of Marper and S, finding that:

> …the blanket and indiscriminate nature of the powers of retention of the fingerprints, cellular samples and DNA profiles of persons suspected but not convicted of offences, as applied in the case of the present applicants, fails to strike a fair balance between the competing public and private interests and that the respondent State has overstepped any acceptable margin of appreciation in this regard.[10]

The case did not focus on whether police had the legal right to obtain the evidence, but whether retaining it breached the right to private life of the individuals concerned, under Article 8 of the Convention, and the right to fair and equal treatment under Article 14. It highlighted what could be considered an unfair distinction between individuals suspected and charged with an offence but subsequently released without conviction; and those in the broader community who had never been suspected of committing, and never been charged with committing a criminal offence.

Following the *Marper* ruling in 2008, the United Kingdom Government responded with a number of policy changes over the following years. The DNA profiles of children younger than 10 were removed from the database and legislative amendments were announced. Individuals convicted of a recordable offence still have their DNA profiles retained indefinitely; however, under the amended legislation, the government committed to, among other measures, deleting the profiles of persons arrested but not convicted of other offences after a specified number years.

In 2020, the decision in *Marper* was reaffirmed in *Gaughran v The United Kingdom*.[11] The European Court of Human Rights, in this case, ruled that the indefinite retention of biometric data (a digital DNA profile, fingerprints, and photographs that could be used for biometric facial recognition) of an individual convicted of a relatively minor offence, was a breach of a person's right to respect for their private life under Article 8 Convention. The government had sought to retain Gaughran's biometric data indefinitely, without any reference to the degree of seriousness of the offence committed or the need for retention, and with no opportunity for review of the decision. The Court held that this approach was unnecessary, failed to strike a

---

[8] *R v Marper & S* (2004) UKHL 39.
[9] *Case of S. and Marper v The United Kingdom* ECtHR, 4 December 2008.
[10] Ibid, 119.
[11] *Case of Gaughran v. The United Kingdom* (Application no. 45245/15) ECtHR, 13 February 2020.

fair balance between the relevant competing public and private interests, and was a disproportionate interference with Gaughran's right to respect for his private life:

> For the reasons set out above, the Court finds that the indiscriminate nature of the powers of retention of the DNA profile, fingerprints and photograph of the applicant as person convicted of an offence, even if spent, without reference to the seriousness of the offence or the need for indefinite retention and in the absence of any real possibility of review, failed to strike a fair balance between the competing public and private interests. The Court recalls its finding that the State retained a slightly wider margin of appreciation in respect of the retention of fingerprints and photographs. However, that widened margin is not sufficient for it to conclude that the retention of such data could be proportionate in the circumstances, which include the lack of any relevant safeguards including the absence of any real review.
> Accordingly, the respondent State has overstepped the acceptable margin of appreciation in this regard and the retention at issue constitutes a disproportionate interference with the applicant's right to respect for private life and cannot be regarded as necessary in a democratic society. There has accordingly been a violation of Article 8 of the Convention.[12]

3.3 Genomics and Forensic Genealogy

The most recent developments in law enforcement use of DNA identification should be understood in the context of corresponding medical advancements. Since the 1990s, genomic medicine has been increasingly important in understanding and treating health conditions, particularly since the completion of the Human Genome Project, by the United States Department of Energy and the National Institutes of Health in 2003, which located and sequenced all human genes (NHGRI, 2019).

Genomics-based predictive health screening to identify predisposition to specific diseases, inform lifestyle choices and improve health outcomes, is now widely available. As is genomics-based ancestry analysis, indicative of the ethnic background or global region a person descends from. Population genome screening programs have been established in a number of countries, steps toward population-wide databases that will further expand medical knowledge and treatment (Feero et al., 2018). Benefits include new therapies and greater understanding of a populations' predisposition to specific diseases, which can inform public health interventions.

Genomic information can not only reveal details of a person's health and susceptibility to disease; but also their ethnic background, paternity and relationship to others. It is also associated with increasingly important issues relating to data security, privacy and trust; and requires ongoing development of standards and frameworks to regulate genomic data sharing (Capps et al., 2013; GALGH, 2019). The *Nuffield Council on Bioethics* has identified scientific developments in genomics, and their relationship to crime and security, as a key issue for society to address this decade (Nuffield Council on Bioethics, 2019). Previously, ethics and regulation in this area has focused on specific technologies, such as gene editing, rather than the regulation of genomic data, which is rapidly growing in importance (Gyngell &

---

[12] Ibid, 96–8.

Savulescu, 2015). While there are existing ethical guidelines and regulation relating to the use of genomic data in clinical practice, there are gaps that may require new approaches to consent to be developed, given that the implications of genomics extend beyond a single individual (Kaye et al., 2015).

Direct-to-consumer (DTC) genomics companies offering mail-order testing, for health diagnosis and ancestry testing, are now widely available on the internet. The largest include 23andMe and Ancestry.com, which offer increasingly accessible pricing structures as the cost of the associated technology decreases. GEDmatch allows users to upload data produced by other companies to search for potential genetic relatives. Consumers of these services receive testing equipment in the mail, undertake their own cheek swab, and return it to the company, which provides the results by email, discarding the biological material but retaining the genomic data. By 2020, more than 15 million people had submitted to Ancestry.com and more than 10 million to 23 and Me (Regalado, 2019).

In this context, cross sector use of genomic health and ancestry data by law enforcement (forensic genealogy) has arisen. If law enforcement conducting an investigation do not obtain a match for a suspect's DNA profile on their national database, and it is a significant crime that warrants the investment of further time and resources, they have, in some instances, resorted to searching the holdings of a commercial genomic database, in an attempt to identify their suspect (Phillips, 2018).

Forensic genealogy involves searching for a potential common ancestor of their suspect who is a consumer of a DTC genomic testing company. It is therefore vastly broader in scope than traditional one-to-one matching against a database of convicted offenders that occurs with searches of established DNA databases. Forensic genealogy enables searching as widely as fourth cousins of the individual donor that submitted their genomic data to a health or ancestry testing company, estimated to be, on average, approximately 100 individuals (Phillips, 2018). Given that more than 26 million people, mostly in the United States, have submitted their genomic data for testing to one of these companies, multiplying that figure by 100 provides an indication of the potential scope of the technique.

There is a detailed process that law enforcement must undertake to identify their suspect on this basis, requiring that a significant number of people be investigated and ruled out. For example, where the genetic match indicated a second cousin relationship, investigators would hypothesise a common set of great-grandparents, and use birth, death and marriage records to construct a family tree of three generations. They would then construct four family trees of the great grandparents, and narrow down the list of grandparents, parents, great uncles and aunts, uncles and aunts, siblings, first and second cousins, on the basis that, for example, some may be deceased, live overseas, or can be excluded based on other data such as age or eyewitness reports – a time consuming task that would only be justified in serious cases. Investigators would then establish a small number of individuals that would then be overtly or covertly investigated, and their DNA sought to directly compare that individual's DNA profile with the crime scene sample (Scudder et al., 2019).

Forensic genealogy is controversial in that it involves the use of genomic data not provided for the purposes of a law enforcement investigation, but by a consumer, seeking to obtain information about their personal health and/or ancestry, who may not have anticipated its use, or capacity to be used for this purpose, nor the significant potential implications for themselves, or a member of their extended family. It is being used as a last resort to identify suspects of serious offences; however, as it lacks legislative backing and regulation, it would be particularly alarming if it became used routinely. Many genomic DTC companies do provide notice in their terms and conditions that genomic information may be used for this purpose. For example, the 23andMe privacy statement provides notice to consumers that they share information, including genomic information, with third parties, as required by 'laws, regulations, judicial or other government subpoenas, warrants, or orders'.[13]

A high profile example of evidence obtained as a result of this technique in the United States is the conviction of former police officer Joseph DeAngelo. DeAngelo was convicted of 13 murders, committed over a twelve year period in the 1970s and 1980s, and has been popularly referred to as the 'golden state killer' (Gold, 2019). Law enforcement reportedly used the GEDmatch site to identify Deangelo after identifying a distant relative of their suspect, and tracing a family tree back to the 1880s, before finally arresting DeAngelo after obtaining DNA from his rubbish and confirming a match. It has been reported that investigators have used GEDmatch in more than 100 investigations in the United States, leading to other arrests (DeLisi, 2018). Those that object to this practice argue that it amounts to a fishing expedition, rather than a targeted and proportionate law enforcement investigation, placing a large number of genetic relatives under suspicion, affecting not only to the individual that submitted their genomic data to the DTC genomics company, but potentially all their genetic relatives (Murphy, 2018).

China established a national DNA database in the early 2000s, incorporating DNA profiles from offenders and suspects in criminal investigations. However, it has recently been reported that over the past 10 years, the Chinese government began collecting DNA profiles from one-in-ten of the male general population, and in some specific areas, 100% of the population (Dirks & Leibold, 2020). China is the world leader in public surveillance, having established a social credit system incorporating a sophisticated data integration program, drawing on, among other sources, CCTV, facial recognition, metadata, financial records and automated number plate recognition (Qiang, 2019). This system detects and implements sanctions on citizens who repeatedly fail to comply with social norms.

It has been reported that in 2013, DNA profiles from all residents of the Tibetan Autonomous Region (approximately 3 million people) were collected, and in 2016, from all residents of the Xinjiang Uyghur Autonomous Region (approximately 23 million) (Dirks & Leibold, 2020).[14] In addition to identification and surveillance; analysis of the genome (DNA phenotyping) can undertaken to determine an

---

[13] 23andMe Privacy Policy, section 2(b)(ii), section 4(e). https://www.23andme.com/en-int/about/privacy/

[14] Other biometrics were also universally collected, including facial, fingerprint and iris templates and voice recordings.

individual's ethnicity – noting that ethnic populations within China, such as the Uyghurs have reportedly been subjected to discriminatory treatment (Qiang, 2019).

The collection of DNA profiles from 10% of males in the general population (equating to approximately 70 million men), including from preschool aged children, began in 2017 (World Bank, 2019). Using the forensic genealogy technique described above, it is possible to identify individuals from whom DNA has *not* been collected, on the basis of their genetic relatedness to individuals who have. Scientific research predicts that universal reach of a population could be achieved using this technique from a DNA database of only 2% of the total population (Scudder et al., 2019). By collecting DNA from 10% of the male population, it is likely that 100% of the Chinese population could be identified using forensic genealogy techniques.

The Chinese Government cites research of Chinese genetics, criminal investigation and missing person cases as a rationale for undertaking this DNA sampling. A translated blood collection notice issued by the Public Security Bureau in Fujian Province states:

> In order to cooperate with the foundational investigative work of the seventh national census and the third generation digital ID cards, our district's public security organs will on the basis of earlier village ancestral genealogical charts, select a representative group of men from whom to collect blood samples. This work will not only help carry on and enhance the genealogical culture of the Chinese people, but will also effectively prevent children and the elderly from going missing, assist in the speedy identification of missing people during various kinds of disasters, help police crack cases, and to the greatest extent retrieve that which is lost for the masses. This is a great undertaking that will benefit current and future generations, and we hope village residents will enthusiastically cooperate (Dirks & Leibold, 2020, 11).

The cross sector use of genomic data from health and ancestry databases for law enforcement purposes raises concerns about the adequacy of existing laws regulating forensic evidence, and overreach by investigators, particularly given the number of people that have submitted their data to these databases, and that it is likely that population wide coverage can be extrapolated, using the forensic genealogy technique. In authoritarian states such as China, the government is taking a more direct approach, obtaining genomic data from a proportion of the population that would also enable the entire population to be identified using the forensic genealogy technique, and in relation to some ethnic subpopulations, establishing universal databases. The ethical implications of these developments will be discussed in the following section.

3.4 Ethical Analysis

The expanding use of DNA/genomic data that has been described above raises a number of pressing ethical concerns. Fundamental moral principles must continue to be valued in liberal democracies, notwithstanding the benefits to individual and public health, and community safety that the unrestrained use of this data may afford. The cross-sector use of genomic data can be understood from the perspectives of individual privacy, autonomy, public safety, and democratic accountability in various domains. These domains include law enforcement, public health, medical research, and private sector commercialization. Central to the ethical, legal and policy issues associated with genomic data is the tension that exists between the legitimate collection of information by law enforcement, health and other government agencies, as well as commercial service provision, on the one hand, and individual rights to privacy and autonomy on the other. In a criminal law and national security context, the threat of terrorism over the past 20 years has resulted in ever greater powers for law enforcement and intelligence agencies (Miller & Walsh, 2016; Miller & Gordon, 2014) to collect evidence and conduct surveillance in order to prevent, detect and disrupt these activities, and these have extended to other forms of crime (Miller, 2009).

It is sometimes assumed that the relationship between, for instance, autonomy and security is a zero-sum relationship and that, therefore, any increase in security that decreases someone's autonomy will necessarily lead to an overall loss in autonomy. This assumption is false; or, at least, it is often false. For instance, if the police have access to the DNA of all persons with a record of having committed serious crimes, then, given that the number of such persons is small but they commit a large percentage of serious crimes, their loss of autonomy in respect of control over their DNA may be more than offset not only by an overall reduction in harm, but also by an overall increase in autonomy. This is because many persons will enjoy an increase in their autonomy, namely those persons who would have been future victims of crime had the offenders in question not been incarcerated for their past crimes, or deterred from future crimes, as a result of criminal investigators' access to the DNA of these offenders. Here it is important to note that serious crimes such as grievous bodily harm, rape and domestic violence are in large part attacks on autonomy. An analogous point concerning an assumed zero-sum relationship can be made in respect of privacy and security, especially when it is taken into account that infringements of privacy can often be mitigated, such as, in the case of law enforcement's use of big-data analytics, by processes of anonymization of data prior to the point of identification of suspects. That said, increases in law enforcement powers, including increased cross-sector genomic data access, have the potential to unacceptably compromise autonomy, privacy, and other liberal democratic principles.

Public safety and security are fundamental values in liberal democracies, as in other polities, including many authoritarian ones. However, liberal democracies are also committed to democracy and individual privacy and autonomy, and, therefore, to democratic accountability (Miller & Gordon, 2014; Miller & Walsh, 2016; Miller & Blackler, 2016). Accordingly, fundamental ethical principles must continue to be valued, notwithstanding the benefits to community safety that access to commercial genomic databases, such as 23andMe or Ancestry.com, can provide by enabling law enforcement to detect and convict perpetrators of serious crimes. While debates will continue between proponents of security, on the one hand, and defenders of privacy, on the other, there is often a lack of clarity in relation to the values or principles allegedly in conflict—these principles and the relationships between them will now be discussed.

The notion of privacy was elaborated in Chap. 2. Let us now apply that notion to the case of genomic data. First, privacy is a right that people have in relation to other persons and organizations with respect to: (a) the possession of information (including genomic data) about themselves by other persons and by organizations, for example personal health, familial and identity information stored in genomic databases; or (b) the observation/perceiving of themselves—including of their movements, relationships and so on—by other persons, for example via law enforcement having access to their genomic data that facilitates linkage with a particular location based on an analysis of biological material deposited at that site (Miller & Gordon, 2014). Genomic data is therefore implicated in both informational and observational concerns.

Second, the right to privacy delimits an informational and observational 'space', namely the private sphere (Miller & Gordon, 2014 Ch. 10; Miller & Blackler, 2016 Ch. 4). This informational space includes genomic data; specifically, the data constituting a person's genome that is particular to that person and, relatedly, a person's DNA profile. However, the right to autonomy consists of a right to decide what to think and do, and the right to control the private sphere. So the right to privacy consists of the right to exclude organizations and other individuals (the right to autonomy) from personal information, such as genomic data.

Naturally, the right to privacy is not absolute; it can be overridden (Miller & Gordon, 2014 Ch. 10; Miller & Blackler, 2016 Ch. 4; Miller & Walsh, 2016). Moreover, its precise boundaries are unclear but, arguably, person has a right that law enforcement agencies not have access to their genomic data, although this right can be overridden under certain circumstances, namely if they have been convicted of a serious crime (their DNA profile will then be included in a forensic database). For instance, this right might be overridden if an individual is reasonably expected of being involved in a crime, and police have a warrant, approval from a judicial officer, legislative authority etc., and then only for the purpose of identifying persons who have committed a specific crime. If persons have committed a serious crime, such as murder or assault, in the past, it would be morally acceptable to utilize the retention of their genomic data (*as it relates to identity, not health conditions*) by including it in a database and matching against samples obtained from crime scenes. This is a specific and targeted measure to improve public safety, and even then, the data can only be used in such a way that has been legislated for by a democratically accountable government. As discussed above, there are already millions of individuals in countries such as Australia, the U.K. and the United States included in forensic DNA databases of this type.

Third, a degree of privacy is necessary in order for people to pursue their personal projects, whatever those projects might be. Thus knowledge of someone else's health status, familial relationships or genomic identity can lead to that information and any associated vulnerabilities being exploited, or otherwise compromised. *Autonomy*—including the exercise of autonomy in the public sphere—requires a measure of privacy.

Thus far we have considered the rights of a *single* individual. However, it is important to consider the implications of the infringement, indeed violation, of the privacy of groups of people and, ultimately, of the whole citizenry by the state (and/or by other powerful institutional actors, such as corporations). Such violations on a large scale can lead to a power imbalance between the state and the citizenry and, thereby, undermine liberal democracy itself.

Accordingly, while it is morally acceptable to access genomic data for necessary circumscribed purposes, such as the provision of healthcare or medical research, or, with the consent of the relevant individuals, for ancestry testing, it would not be acceptable to collect this data in an indiscriminate manner without consent and with no legal authority, to investigate crime. However, the DNA profiles of convicted offenders on forensic DNA databases are, and arguably ought to be, available for law enforcement purposes, for example to assist in the investigation of serious crimes. The issue that then arises is the determination of the point on the spectrum at which privacy and security considerations are appropriately balanced.

In light of our notion of privacy, we are entitled to conclude that some form of it is a constitutive human good (Miller & Walsh, 2016). As such, infringements of privacy ought to be avoided. That said, as mentioned above, privacy can reasonably be overridden by security considerations under some circumstances, such as when lives are at risk. After all, the right to life is, in general, a weightier moral right than the right to privacy. Thus, utilizing genomic data in a forensic DNA database or from a suspect to investigate a serious crime such as a murder, if conducted under warrant or legislative provisions, is surely ethically justified. On the other hand, intrusive access to the genomic data of individuals, collected for another purpose, where those individuals have not had any contact with the criminal justice system, and the data was obtained without any legal authority, particularly in relation to relatively minor offences such as theft, is far less likely to be justified. Moreover, given the importance of, so to speak, the aggregate privacy of the citizenry, relatively small-scale threats to public safety are unlikely to be of sufficient weight to justify substantial infringements of privacy, for example unregulated access to the genomic relationships of millions of people by law enforcement agencies. Furthermore, regulation and associated accountability mechanisms need to be in place to ensure that, for instance, a genomic database created for a legitimate purpose, for example health or ancestry testing with the express consent of the individuals involved, is not accessed, except with the appropriate legal authority and in relation to the investigation of serious crimes.

Here we need again to stress the particular significance of genomic data but now elaborate on the reasons for this. Genomic data, and DNA profiles in particular, are (in effect, namely for our purposes here and, therefore, issues of gene-editing aside) unchanging and unalterable; therefore, they are a reliable life-long identifier. This means that they have greater utility for law enforcement than do other forms of personal data. However, it also means that there is much more at stake in terms of an individual's privacy and autonomy should this genomic data be provided to law enforcement or other agencies (including private sector ones). Moreover, the genome of a person is constitutive of that person's individual-specific (biological) identity. Accordingly, the threshold for the infringement of an individual's right to control access to their genomic data is higher than it is for most other personal information. And there is a further point here. For the genome of a person is not only constitutive of that person's individual-specific (biological) identity, that same genome is *in part* constitutive of the individual-specific (biological) identity of the person's relatives (to a decreasing extent depending on the degree of relatedness; for example a sibling is more related than a second cousin). Accordingly, there is a species of joint right to control genomic data in play here, and not merely an exclusively individual right.

3.4.1 Joint Rights to Genomic Data

Joint rights are rights that attach to individual persons but do so jointly (Miller, 1999, 2001a Ch. 7, 2003, 2010 Ch. 2). Thus, roughly speaking, two or more agents have the right to some good if they each have a right to that good, no-one else has a right to that good, and if the individual right of one of these persons to the good is dependent on the individual rights of the others to the good. The right to control one's genome data needs to be regarded, we suggest, as a (qualified) joint right; that is, as a right jointly held with the individual's relatives. [15] If these rights are, as we are suggesting, joint rights, then it follows that an individual may not have an exclusive individual right to provide his or her genomic data to direct-to-consumer genetic testing providers, or to law enforcement. Of course, when it comes to serious crimes, the consent of an individual regarding access to his or her genomic data is not necessarily required, for example if the individual is a past offender and hence his or her genomic data in the form of a DNA profile is held in a law enforcement database. However, in cases where identifying the person who has committed a crime relies on the genomic data of relatives known to be innocent, and the relatives in question have a joint right to the data in question, then it may be that *all* of these relatives need to have consented to the collection of the genomic data in question.[16] For in voluntarily providing their DNA to law enforcement, a person is, in effect, providing law enforcement with the partially overlapping DNA data of their relatives. But presumably a person does not have a moral right to decide to provide law enforcement with another person's DNA data. Accordingly, it seems that a person, A, does not have a moral right to *unilaterally* provide law enforcement with his or her own data, namely A's DNA data, given that in doing so A is providing to law enforcement the partially overlapping DNA data of A's relatives, B, C, D etc. Rather, A, B, C, D etc. have an (admittedly qualified) joint moral right to the DNA data in

---

[15] It is a qualified joint right given that the genomic data of any one of the persons is not identical to the genome data of the other persons, that is, the sets of genomic data are overlapping.

[16] This consent issue adds to other problems that exist with direct-to-consumer genetic testing, such as the accuracy of the tests and the fact that the results are not provided in a clinical setting by a healthcare professional.

question, and, therefore, the right (being a joint right) has to be exercised jointly; that is, perhaps all (or most) have to agree. Naturally, as is the case with individual moral rights, joint moral rights can be overridden. For instance, A's individual right to know whether he is vulnerable to a hereditary disease might justify his providing his genomic data to health authorities and doing so without the consent of any of his relatives. Again, the joint moral right of a group of persons to refuse to provide law enforcement with the DNA data in a murder investigation, for instance, may well be overridden by their collective moral responsibility to assist the police.

3.4.2 Collective Moral Responsibility to Assist Law Enforcement

Evidently, strategies for combating crime involve a complex set of often competing, and sometimes interconnected moral considerations (e.g. some privacy rights, such as control over personal data, are as we saw above themselves aspects of autonomy); so hard choices have to be made. However, the idea of a collective responsibility on the part of individuals to jointly suffer some costs, e.g. loss of privacy rights, in favour of a collective good (prosecuting serious crime) lies at the heart of all such effective strategies (Miller, 2001a, pp. 148–150, 2010, pp. 337–8). Accordingly, we need an analysis of the appropriate notion of collective responsibility. The notion of collective responsibility in question was elaborated in Chap. 1, i.e. collective responsibility as joint responsibility (Miller, 2001a Ch. 8, 2020 Ch. 4, 2001b, 2006, 2014, 2015, 2018).

Let us now apply this concept of collective moral responsibility to access to genomic information by law enforcement agencies to investigate and prosecute crime and, in particular, to population wide DNA databases (Miller, 2018). Certainly, there is a collective good (Miller, 2003, 2010 Ch. 2) to which, let us assume, the use of this information will make a significant contribution to law enforcement, namely, the investigation and prosecution of serious crimes and the prevention of harm and preservation of the lives of those who may otherwise have been harmed if a serial killer or rapist is not brought to justice as swiftly as possible. Naturally, those whose lives would not have otherwise been preserved receive a benefit, namely, their life that those who would not have been impacted do not receive. Moreover, crime imposes economic and social costs for society that affect individuals more broadly than those who are directly victimised by crime.

As stated above, there is a collective moral responsibility of joint rights holders of DNA to provide this DNA to law enforcement, at least in the case of serious crimes. That is, their joint moral right is overridden by their collective moral responsibility. However, this collective moral responsibility applies in specific cases on a piecemeal basis; it is not a collective moral responsibility to provide their DNA data in a manner that contributes to a population wide DNA database. Moreover, it is not a collective moral responsibility to provide their DNA data on a permanent basis.

Rather they have a joint moral right that the data be destroyed upon the conclusion of the specific criminal investigation and associated trial.

3.5 Conclusion

We have described DNA identification, and the recent development of cross-sector access of genomic data, collected for health and ancestry purposes, by law enforcement for criminal investigation purposes. It is likely that these practices, which have been documented in the United States, are also being undertaken in other liberal democracies, such as Australia and the U.K., although there is not currently any publicly available data to support this. In light of these developments, we have outlined the relevant ethical principles and identified a number of actual or potential problems that arise.

The issues in this area cannot be framed in terms of a simple weighing of, let alone trade-off between, individual privacy rights versus the community's interest in public safety. The issues are far more ethically complex, and we conclude with three general points.

First, law enforcement access to and searching of the genomic data of citizens, held by private companies and created for specific purposes, without legislative oversight or regulation, and the utilization of this data in investigations, infringes privacy rights and joint moral rights to genomic data, has the potential to create a power imbalance between governments and citizens, and risks undermining important principles hitherto taken to be constitutive of the liberal democratic state, such as that an individual has the right to freedom from state interference absent prior evidence of violation by that individual of its laws, subject to transparent and appropriately justified exceptions. That said, citizens have a collective moral responsibility to assist law enforcement (assuming in doing so they are not violating the moral rights of fellow citizens).

Second, as part of the introduction of laws to regulate this activity, if these laws are deemed to be justified, the cross-sector use of genomic data in this way must be clearly and demonstrably justified in terms of efficiency and effectiveness in law enforcement investigations, and its use circumscribed accordingly, rather than by general appeal to community security or safety.

Finally, in so far as the use of genomic data created for health or ancestry purposes can be justified for the investigation of serious crimes, and privacy and other concerns mitigated, it is imperative that this use be regulation by appropriate criminal procedure legislation, and subject to accountability mechanisms to guard against misuse. Moreover, the citizenry should be aware of these applications–genomic data should only be used for specific, justified purposes, backed by legislation, and subject to judicial review.

References

Australian Criminal Intelligence Commission (ACIC). (2021). *Biometric and forensic services.* https://www.acic.gov.au/our-services/biometric-and-forensic-services

Capps, B., et al. (2013). *Imagined futures: Capturing the benefits of genome sequencing for society.* HUGO Committee on Ethics, Law and Society.

DeLisi, M. (2018). Forensic epidemiology harnessing the power of public DNA sources to capture career criminals. *Forensic Science International, 291,* 20–21.

Dirks, E., & Leibold, J. (2020). *Genomic surveillance: Inside China's DNA dragnet* (Policy Brief Report No. 34/2020). Australian Strategic Policy Institute.

Federal Bureau of Investigation. (2021). *NDIS statistics.* https://www.fbi.gov/services/laboratory/biometric-analysis/codis/ndis-statistics

Feero, F., et al. (2018). Precision medicine, genome sequencing, and improved population health. *Journal of the American Medical Association, 319,* 1979–1980.

Global Alliance for Linked Genomics and Health (GALGH). (2019). *Enabling responsible linked genomic data sharing for the benefit of human health.* https://www.ga4gh.org

Gold, R. (2019). From swabs to handcuffs: How commercial DNA services can expose you to criminal charges. *California Western Law Review, 55,* 491–519.

Gyngell, C., & Savulescu, J. (2015). The medical case for gene editing. *Ethics in Biology, Engineering and Medicine, 6,* 57–66.

Jobling, M., & Gill, P. (2004). Encoded evidence: DNA in forensic analysis. *Nature Reviews Genetics, 5,* 739–751.

Kaye, J., et al. (2015). Dynamic consent: A patient interface for twenty-first century research networks. *European Journal of Human Genetics, 23,* 141–146.

Miller, S. (1999). Collective rights. *Public Affairs Quarterly, 1*(4), 331–346.

Miller, S. (2001a). *Social action: A teleological account.* Cambridge University Press.

Miller, S. (2001b). Collective responsibility and omissions. *Business and Professional Ethics, 20*(1), 5–24.

Miller, S. (2003). Institutions, collective goods and individual rights. *Protosociology, 18,* 184–207.

Miller, S. (2006). Collective moral responsibility: An individualist account. *Midwest Studies in Philosophy, XXX,* 176–193.

Miller, S. (2009). *Terrorism and counter-terrorism: Ethics and liberal democracy.* Blackwell.

Miller, S. (2010). *The moral foundations of social institutions: A philosophical study.* Cambridge University Press.

Miller, S. (2014). Police detectives, criminal investigations and collective responsibility. *Criminal Justice Ethics, 33*(1), 21–39.

Miller, S. (2015). Joint epistemic action and collective responsibility. *Social Epistemology, 29*(3), 280–302.

Miller, S. (2018). Joint epistemic action: Some applications. *Journal of Applied Philosophy, 35*(2), 300–318.

Miller, S. (2020). Freedom of political communication, propaganda and the role of epistemic institutions. In M. Christen, B. Gordjin, & M. Loi (Eds.), *Ethics of Cybersecurity.* Springer.

Miller, S., & Blackler, J. (2016). *Ethical issues in policing.* Routledge.

Miller, S., & Gordon, I. (2014). *Investigative ethics: Ethics for police detectives and criminal investigators* (1st Edn.). Blackwell.

Miller, S., & Walsh, P. (2016). NSA, Snowden and the ethics and accountability of intelligence gathering. In J. Galliott & J. Reed (Eds.), *Ethics and the future of spying: Technology, intelligence collection and national security* (pp. 193–204). Routledge.

Murphy, E. (2018). Law and policy oversight of familial searches in recreational genealogy databases. *Forensic Science International, 292,* 5–9.

National Human Genome Research Institute (NHGRI). (2019). *A brief guide to genomics.* https://www.genome.gov/about-genomics/fact-sheets/A-Brief-Guide-to-Genomics

References

Nuffield Council on Bioethics. (2019). *Horizon scanning workshops*. Retrieved from https://nuffieldbioethics.org/future-work/horizon-scanning-workshops

Phillips, C. (2018). The Golden State Killer investigation and the nascent field of forensic genealogy. *Forensic Science International: Genetics, 36*, 186–188.

Qiang, X. (2019). The road to digital unfreedom: President Xi's surveillance state. *Journal of Democracy, 30*, 53–67.

Regalado, A. (2019, February 11). More than 26 million people have taken an at-home ancestry test. *MIT Technology Review*. https://www.technologyreview.com/2019/02/11/103446/more-than-26-million-people-have-taken-an-at-home-ancestry-test/

Scudder, N., et al. (2019). Policy and regulatory implications of the new frontier of forensic genomics: Direct-to-consumer genetic data and genealogy records. *Current Issues in Criminal Justice, 31*, 194–216.

Smith, M. (2016). *DNA evidence in the Australian legal system*. Lexis Nexis.

Smith, M. (2018). Universal forensic DNA databases: Balancing the costs and benefits. *Alternative Law Journal, 43*(2), 131–135.

United Kingdom Government Official Statistics. (2021). *National DNA database statistics*. https://www.gov.uk/government/statistics/national-dna-database-statistics

World Bank. (2019). *Population total: China*. https://data.worldbank.org/indicator/SP.POP.TOTL?locations=CN

Open Access This chapter is licensed under the terms of the Creative Commons Attribution 4.0 International License (http://creativecommons.org/licenses/by/4.0/), which permits use, sharing, adaptation, distribution and reproduction in any medium or format, as long as you give appropriate credit to the original author(s) and the source, provide a link to the Creative Commons license and indicate if changes were made.

The images or other third party material in this chapter are included in the chapter's Creative Commons license, unless indicated otherwise in a credit line to the material. If material is not included in the chapter's Creative Commons license and your intended use is not permitted by statutory regulation or exceeds the permitted use, you will need to obtain permission directly from the copyright holder.

Chapter 4
Biometric and Non-biometric Integration: Dual Use Dilemmas

Abstract Biometric identification is now closely integrated with other forms of data, data systems and communications technologies, such as smartphones, metadata and social media, and as the key security feature on smartphones, and by extension, social media accounts, online profiles and identity. For this reason, we consider the interaction between biometric and other forms of identification data, and data systems, building upon the consideration of the main biometrics in the first three chapters. We begin with a general discussion of data systems and integration. This is followed by a discussion of the interrelationship with biometrics, and broader significance of, metadata, smartphone applications and social media. In combination with biometric identification technologies, these provide detailed insights into individuals' activities and behaviours. The ethical analysis in this chapter focuses on dual use dilemmas. Roughly speaking, dual use dilemmas in science and technology arise in virtue of the fact that such science and technology can be used to greatly benefit humankind, but also, unfortunately, to cause great harm to humankind. Consider, for instance, nuclear science and technology. It can be used as a cheap and peaceful energy source, or to build nuclear weapons. Similarly, facial recognition technology could be used by police only to track persons guilty of serious crimes; or it could be used to monitor ordinary citizens' behaviour by an authoritarian government.

Keywords Biometric identification · Data integration · Big data · Artificial intelligence (AI) · Metadata · Smartphones · Dual use dilemma

4.1 Data Systems and Integration

Over the past 30 years, digitalisation, data analytics and integration has changed the way law enforcement agencies approach criminal investigation, in comparison with traditional information systems –paper-based file and index catalogue systems that required a large amount of storage space, were time consuming to interrogate, and allowed little scope for information sharing outside specific jurisdictions or commands. Just as fingerprint identification moved from manual comparison of ink prints on cards, to digitalised algorithmic based data systems, so has all other forms of administrative and intelligence data. Similar issues in relation to efficiency, accuracy and data integrity are relevant across these different data systems. Databases are now widely used by law enforcement to store and compare information about crime scenes, individuals and networks. These range from record management systems, to complex analytical software systems that inform tactical and strategic intelligence (Ratcliffe, 2008). While publicly available data on the impact these databases have on investigation outcomes is limited due to sensitivities associated with the nature of the information, there is evidence indicating that these systems can improve policing through the analysis of data, improving the speed of detection, and assisting strategic planning (Koper et al., 2014).

Biometric and other forms of law enforcement data systems have been introduced around the world. In the United States, the Science and Technology Branch of the Federal Bureau of Investigation (FBI) is responsible for the development and maintenance of national police information systems. The Criminal Justice Information System (CJIS) is the central repository of criminal justice information, for the FBI and the other United States federal, state and local law enforcement agencies. United States databases include the National Crime Information Center (NCIC), the National Instant Criminal Background Check System (NICBCS), the Combined DNA Index System (CODIS) and the National Integrated Ballistics Information Network (NIBIN) (Federal Bureau of Investigation, 2021).

In the United Kingdom, the Home Office and the Association for Police and Crime Commissioners manage Britain's police information systems. Current databases include the Police National Database (PND), the Police National Computer (PNC), the National DNA Database (NDNAD), the National fingerprint and identity platform database (IDENT1), and the National Ballistics Intelligence Services (NABIS).

The Australian Criminal Intelligence Commission (ACIC) was formed in 2016 following a merge between the Australian Crime Commission (ACC) and the CrimTrac Agency. CrimTrac had been responsible for the development, sharing and maintenance of law enforcement databases in Australia since July, 2000, while the ACC was the a federal agency established to investigate organised crime. According to the ACIC, its databases seek to enhance Australian policing and law enforcement, and '…contribute directly to the effectiveness and efficiency of police and law enforcement agencies in Australia' (ACIC, 2021). In addition to DNA and fingerprints, the ACIC administers national databases relating to ballistics, cybercrime reports, firearms ownership, vehicles and persons of interest (ACIC, 2021).

A range of issues can impact the effectiveness of police information systems such as poor implementation and underutilisation of the databases, as well as a lack of training. Data security, missing or inaccurate data (completeness and validity), siloed information, ineffective human-computer interfaces, poor search capabilities and hardware limits need to be considered and managed when implementing new information systems into police agencies and practices (Koper et al., 2014).

4.1 Data Systems and Integration

As its potential to solve complex problems efficiently becomes increasingly apparent, law enforcement and intelligence agencies are collecting and analysing an increasing volume of data about individuals, in order to prevent and investigate crime. Big data analytics uses tools, techniques and technologies to store, manage and efficiently process this expanding amount and range of data currently being generated. It is characterised by features such as volume, velocity and variety (Pramanik et al., 2017). Identifying the network structures of criminals and inferring their roles can assist law enforcement and intelligence agencies to prevent crime. This can be achieved by mining social media data from sites such as Facebook (which as discussed in Chap. 2, can include biometric facial templates) (Tan et al., 2013). Because it is likely that criminal activities will become increasingly digitised, law enforcement and security agencies are expanding their use of data mining techniques. The proliferation of digitalised data means that it is possible to merge diverse data sets into integrated systems, to enable cross referencing and searching. In contrast, with the previous approach, requiring officers to individually search 'siloed' databases of criminal history, car licence plates etc., intelligence analysts can now interrogate one integrated system that integrates disparate data sources:

> This integration facilitates one of the most transformative features of the big data landscape: the creep of criminal justice surveillance into other, non–criminal justice institutions. Function creep – the phenomenon of data originally collected for one purpose being used for another – contributes to a substantial increase in the data police have access to. Indeed, law enforcement is following an institutional data imperative, securing routine access to a wide range of data on everyday activities from non-police databases (Brayne, 2017).

Palantir is one example of a private sector data integration platform widely used by law enforcement and intelligence agencies around the world. It provides for a tagging system that enables users to visualise and map data, by labelling and linking persons, objects and entities, such as phone numbers, cars, photos, email addresses, social media accounts, metadata, biometric database profiles, and intelligence reports, establishing inter-relationships. Another example is the Enterprise Master Person Index (EMPI), developed by Los Angeles County, that links an individual's interactions with social security, healthcare and law enforcement agencies in order to improve government service delivery (Brayne, 2017).

There are a number of challenges associated with the increasing utilisation and integration of data, and the first point that should be noted is data security. New approaches to consent, management and data protection may be needed to deal with the rapid expansion in the volume and type of data available, and the myriad ways in which it is being used (Kaye et al., 2015). Cases of hacking and significant data breaches involving institutions, governments and businesses are becoming more common (ANU, 2019). The capacity to integrate biometrics, metadata, financial, medical and tax data, adds to these concerns. The use of identification technologies in China to construct a social credit system (discussed further in Chap. 5), demonstrate a potential development of biometric and other data integration in liberal democracies, absent appropriate regulation.

Biometric technologies are an important part of a broader shift taking place in society towards automated decision-making processes that involve more limited human intervention. Artificial intelligence (AI) and deep learning (DL) algorithms are rapidly becoming an important application in relation to biometric data, and a range of other fields, including clinical medicine, finance and government administration. AI refers to computer systems that perform tasks traditionally associated with human intelligence. The algorithms recognise patterns, conduct abstract reasoning and learn from prior examples to undertake pattern recognition tasks (Smith & Heath Jeffery, 2020). There are challenges associated with implementing AI systems in any field because it is not possible to understand precisely how an algorithm arrives at a particular conclusion – described as the problem of black box data processing. Human decision making is complex and often requires contextual knowledge and experience. Continued human oversight is crucial in verifying the accuracy and safety of AI applications in order to facilitate their integration over time. Further, quality standards for implementation, and ensuring AI data is continually evaluated as part of the decision-making process, will be important in preventing and mitigating potential errors. Moreover, from a legal perspective, who will be responsible for errors that occur with the application of AI technology remains unclear. As regulation is developed, it will need to be determined to what extent humans that oversee the technology; institutions that use the software; and the algorithm developers will bear liability. Given the complexity of AI technology, determining where the error occurred, and who is responsible, may be difficult to ascertain.

The challenge of regulating biometric data is part of a broader issue of technology regulation. New technology offers great potential for efficiencies and economic growth, but complex problems associated with privacy, accuracy and data security is an ongoing concern. Effective technology regulation requires an understanding of the relevant science and what the implications are for the individual and society; ethics and regulatory theory, to determine why it should be regulated; and an understanding of legal and parliamentary processes, to determine how it should be regulated. Technology is continually adapting, advancing, and being integrated with new capabilities and applications. Holistic approaches to technology regulation, across a number of sectors, rather than siloed approaches will be most effective over time.

Government agencies today have much greater powers to collect evidence and conduct surveillance to detect and disrupt threats like terrorism and transnational crime (Walsh & Miller, 2016). More proactive collection of data, including biometric information, from citizens who have not committed a crime has become increasingly common, –facilitated by the exponential increase in data created by consumers of services provided by technology and social media companies.

4.1.1 Metadata

Metadata is data that provides information about, or describes, other data. For example, metadata about a text message, may include the phone numbers and type of phones it was sent and received from, their location, and the time and date it was sent–but not the content of the text message itself (Sarre, 2017). The advent of smartphones, which today individuals carry on their person almost everywhere, vastly increased the availability of metadata. Biometrics, in providing access to smartphones, are intrinsically linked to this metadata. Metadata generated by smartphones and internet activity is collected by technology companies for advertising purposes, and many liberal democratic countries now require it to be retained for several years in case it is required in a law enforcement investigation. It is arguably the most significant other form of identification technology at the present time in terms of providing insights into individuals' lives. Integrating metadata with the biometrics discussed throughout this text: biometric data used by technology companies (e.g., facial image access to devices or services); government service provision (e.g., CCTV, passports); and law enforcement (e.g., DNA evidence and facial recognition) allows a very thorough picture of an individual's identity and daily activity can be achieved. The scope of this continues to expand as new devices and applications become available (Sarre, 2017).

The use of metadata and social media by governments was at the heart of Snowden leaks in 2013 (Walsh & Miller, 2016). These leaks provided details of global surveillance programs run by the National Security Agency in the United States, and the Five Eyes intelligence network that collected 'almost anything done on the internet' through confidential agreements with technology companies (Dencik & Cable, 2017). In the time that has passed since, many countries have passed legislation that requires technology companies to store metadata for a number of years and provide it to government agencies if it is deemed necessary for a law enforcement investigation.[1] Some countries have even legislated to prevent encryption hindering law enforcement agencies from accessing metadata.[2]

Australian legislation introduced in 2017 provides a useful example of laws that were introduced following the Snowden leaks.[3] These state that, while a warrant is necessary to obtain the content of communications, metadata can be accessed without a warrant if it is deemed reasonably necessary for an investigation. Telecommunications service providers are required to retain Australian's metadata for two years in order to ensure that it is available for law enforcement investigations if required.[4]

The legislation that facilitates metadata retention is the *Telecommunications (Interception and Access) Amendment (Data Retention) Act 2015* (Cth). It came into effect in October 2015, with telecommunication service providers given until April

---

[1] E.g. in Australia, the *Telecommunications (Interception and Access) Amendment (Data Retention) Act 2015* (Cth) gave telecommunication service providers given until 2017 to establish infrastructure to retain customers' metadata. Section 172 of the legislation states that disclosure of 'the contents or substance of a communication' is not permitted. Details of the kinds of metadata telecommunications service providers are required to retain are provided in section 187AA of the legislation.

[2] Australia enacted (world first legislation) the *Telecommunications and Other Legislation Amendment (Assistance and Access) Act* 2018 (Cth).

[3] *Telecommunications (Interception and Access) Amendment (Data Retention) Act 2015* (Cth).

[4] Ibid, section 172.

2017 to develop infrastructure to retain customers' metadata for the two year period and deliver it to government agencies upon request. While section 187AA of the legislation defines metadata, one aspect that the legislation is unclear on is whether the URLs of websites visited when browsing the internet are considered metadata, which remains unresolved:

> ...metadata (in the context of web browsing) is what remains of a communication or document after its contents and substance is excluded. As a result, the legal definition of metadata is ambiguous; an oversight commentators suggest is surprising. In part, the ambiguity arises from conflicting views on what constitutes 'the content' of a communication. For example, one of the most contentious issues of the current Australian regime is whether URLs are metadata. If they are, then warrantless governmental access to individuals' web browsing history is possible. One view is that as URLs are user-generated, they are content. Another view – expressed by the Attorney-General's Department – is that metadata is 'information that allows a communication to occur'. As that is what URLs do, consequently they are not content. The issue is that that some URLs can identify the substance of a communication (Murphy, 2014).

In Australia, metadata can be accessed without a warrant and there is a relatively low threshold for access. There is only a requirement that it be reasonable necessary for the enforcement of a law imposing a pecuniary penalty or for the protection of the public revenue.[5] It appears that in the years since the metadata legislation was introduced, the number of requests to access it increase each year, as well as the number of government agencies that are permitted to access it. While this type of legislation is passed with politicians discussing the threat of terrorism and its need in that context, over time it is clear that comprises a small proportion of the types of investigations for which it is being used (Redrup, 2019).

Law enforcement may be able to access full content of data held on smartphones with a warrant; however, their ability to do so may be constrained by technical capability i.e. through encryption. A high-profile example of this occurred in the United States in 2016. Apple was ordered by a federal court to 'assist law enforcement agents in enabling the search' of an iPhone seized in relation to a shooting in San Bernardino, California, by unlocking it (Pollack, 2019).[6] Apple resisted this request and publicised the issue, with the CEO Tim Cook declaring the company's opposition and calling for public discussion of the issue of data security. Apple argued that creating a back door into their phone system would weaken their security system for all users, and refused. It was later revealed that the FBI used an Australian firm Azimuth, to break the encryption and access the phone (Nakashima & Albergotti, 2021).

---

[5] Section 179(3).

[6] Order Compelling Apple, Inc to Assist Agents in Search, In re Search of an Apple iPhone Seized during Execution of a Search Warrant on a Black Lexus IS300, California License Plate 35KGD203, No 15-0451, *1 (CD Cal filed Feb 16, 2016) cited in Michael C. Pollack, 'Taking Data' (2019) 86 *University of Chicago Law Review* 77

Australia has enacted legislation facilitating access by law enforcement and national security agencies to encrypted content.[7] This was controversial, although encryption can be used by criminals to communicate and carry out crime, and prevent law enforcement agencies from investigating them or obtaining evidence, it also has legitimate uses, such as securing financial transactions and protected communications (such as between a lawyer and their client). The *Telecommunications and Other Legislation Amendment (Assistance and Access) Act* 2018 (Cth) requires technology companies to provide reasonable assistance to access the content of communications facilitated by their platforms. Under the legislation, technology companies may be required to respond to the following:

- A technical assistance request (TAR): a request that they voluntarily assist law enforcement by providing the technical details about one of their products or services;
- A technical assistance notice (TAN): a requirement that they assist by decrypting a specific communication, or face a fine if they refuse; or
- A technical capability notice (TCN): a requirement that they create a new function to enable police to access a suspect's data, or face a fine if they refuse.[8]

Decision-makers must be satisfied that the request or requirement is reasonable and proportionate and that compliance is practicable and technically feasible.[9] In addition to privacy issues, stakeholders in the technology industry are concerned that creating vulnerabilities in their systems that would compromise their ability to provide their services to their customers, and impact on the commercial viability of Australian companies in the international marketplace. While the legislation was amended to expressly provide that companies 'must not be requested or required to implement or build a systemic weakness or systemic vulnerability';[10] there remain concerns in the technology sector and community about these laws.[11]

A law enforcement operation to access encrypted smartphone communications between 2018 and 2021, led by the FBI and Australian Federal Police, was recently revealed. The Trojan Shield/Operation Ironside operation involved police developing an 'encrypted' messaging app, called ANOM, and marketing this to organised crime groups via undercover agents. The app had a back door that could be accessed by law enforcement and provided a wealth of information and understanding of criminal networks over several years, before being revealed in 2021 and leading to the arrest of more than 800 people worldwide (Pannett & Birnbaum, 2021). This

---

[7] Encryption is the process of encoding messages so that their content can only be read by those that send and receive them.
[8] Defined in *Telecommunications and Other Legislation Amendment (Assistance and Access) Act* 2018 (Cth), section 317B.
[9] Section 317JAA (TARs); section 317P (TANs); and section 317TAAA(6) (TCNs).
[10] Section 317ZG.
[11] *Questions on Notice from Senetas Corporation*, Parliamentary Joint Committee on Intelligence and Security, Review of the Telecommunications and Other Legislation Amendment (Assistance and Access) Bill 2018 (Parliament of Australia, 2018).

development highlights the increasing sophistication and audacity on the part of law enforcement agencies to access communications data that they believe is relevant to investigations, and prevent technology from being used to facilitate organised crime.

4.1.2 Smartphone Applications

Fingerprint and facial recognition biometrics are now widely used to identify and grant access to a smartphone. Due to the high level of security these biometrics provide, possession of a smartphone registered to a specific person has become a proxy for the identity or location of that person (Smith & Urbas, 2021). For example, a smartphone can now be used as a tap and pay device, in the same way as a credit or debit card has been used in the past, it can be used to record the presence of a person at a location, using quick response (QR) code scanning, and provides access to social media and other online accounts.

The accuracy and security of biometric identification technologies have enabled smartphones to become an extension of the physical self for identification purposes. This development was widely observed in relation to government responses to the COVID-19 pandemic. This significant threat to public health, the economy and national security around the world, in 2020 alone, it infected more than 60 million people worldwide, and killed more than 1.5 million (WHO, 2020). Governments adapted existing technologies to inform decision making and improve contact tracing of those who contracted COVID-19 in order to limit the spread of the disease. A range of surveillance technologies can potentially assist with contact tracing, including closed-circuit television cameras, facial recognition technology, thermal imaging cameras, location metadata, automated numberplate recognition and financial transaction data (Servick, 2020).

Given the wide use of smartphones, several countries used metadata to geolocate individuals, while others developed specific apps that the population was required to download which communicate with surrounding phones via Bluetooth, in order to identify other persons that an infected individual has been in close contact with. Technology applications generate information to inform the community and allow them to make decisions that reduce their chance of contracting the virus. This can be an alternative to, or used in conjunction with, lockdowns and curfews, to prevent community transmission of the virus. In both cases, it was argued that the seriousness of the pandemic overrode individual autonomy rights. In South Korea metadata tracking was used to inform community announcements about the movements of individuals who had contracted the virus. The government actually published anonymised maps of the locations those who had contracted COVID-19 visited (Servick, 2020).

China was the country of origin for COVID-19 as well as being the leader in public surveillance (Wang, 2020). As will be discussed further in the following chapter, China has established a social credit system that uses big data integration to profile citizens, and impose sanctions if they repeatedly fail to comply with government policies. The country was well placed to implement technology based public health surveillance systems. The Chinese smartphone application that was introduced in response to the COVID-19 pandemic was known as *Health Code*, and available via the Alipay and WeChat platforms. The application has be described as follows:

> People first fill in their personal information, including their ID number, where they live, whether they have been with people carrying the virus, and their symptoms. The app then churns out one of three colors: green means they can go anywhere, yellow and red mean seven and 14 days of quarantine, respectively. The app also surreptitiously collects – and shares with the police – people's location data (Wang, 2020).

The application has more than 700 million users, who are required to show the colour it displays when they, for example, enter residential areas, shopping centres or public transport, and verify their identity with facial recognition technology. An issue that has caused some debate in China, is that the algorithm that determines the colour allocation has not been disclosed, so individuals do not know what has caused them to receive a yellow or red rating, with those affected criticising this as being ruled by machines (Wang, 2020). There have also been indications that the application will remain in place after the pandemic has ended, for ongoing public health monitoring and health care service provision, further expanding the already extensive government surveillance infrastructure (Sheng & Zijia, 2020).

Bluetooth technology does not monitor an individual's location and applications of this type have been introduced by governments in Australia, Singapore, among others, and have been largely accepted in those countries, although ultimately proved not to be effective for contact tracing purposes and were replaced with other measures, such as QR code scanning upon entry to locations such as shops and workplaces (Bogle, 2020). Metadata based COVID-19 contract tracing has been more controversial – it can track a person's location whenever their phone is in their possession.[12] In addition to South Korea, metadata has also been used in Israel, where it was reported that a database of citizens' metadata compiled by security agency Shin Bet was being used for contact tracing purposes (Halbfinger et al., 2020). In Norway, the COVID-19 tracing application, *Smittestopp*, which utilised metadata and Bluetooth technology, was criticised by the national data protection agency for its impact on privacy and ultimately suspended (Guardian, 2020).

Security threats are used by governments to make effective claims about necessary measures to address the threats and take exceptional actions beyond what would normally be acceptable (Williams, 2003). As was also relevant to the metadata discussion, the security rationale used in relation to COVID-19 has been repeated used in the past (e.g., counter terrorism), to introduce more extensive data collection practices and associated legislation. There is potential for the collection of data for public health purposes to continue after the threat has passed as part of an ongoing preventative, just as measures to combat the heightened risk of terrorism

---

[12] As noted above, metadata refers to information such as the location of the devices used, the phone numbers involved in a communication, and the date and time of the communication.

after 9/11 became later employed against serious crime, and then against less serious crime. Metadata collection expanded from initially being used by only select law enforcement and security agencies to being used more widely across government (Smith & Urbas, 2021). Function creep is an important issue to consider in relation to identification technology regulation. Democratic governments should ensure that data is collected for a specific purpose, particularly where it is undertaken in response to extraordinary circumstances such as 9/11 or COVID-19, it is vital that it not used for purposes beyond those intended when the laws were enacted. The technology sector is rapidly growing, with new applications becoming available each year. Potential outcomes of unchecked use of surveillance technologies in liberal democracies is illustrated by the extensive data systems established in China, and in particular their use in relation to ethnic minorities.

4.1.3 Social Media

As noted above, biometric fingerprint and facial recognition, in regulating access to smartphones, simultaneously provide access to social media accounts, and are therefore key indicators of a person's identity in online environments. Facial recognition is widely used to identify and link individuals within social media platforms, such as Facebook's tagging feature (Smith & Urbas, 2021). Biometrics are therefore closely associated with the developments in social media that have significantly influenced the society over the past decade, and they will continue to be central as these applications continue to expand, as well as to future regulatory approaches.

Social media does not include all online websites, but involves a degree of interaction between participants, and collaboration in a non-hierarchical way. It enables users to post self-generated content, such as text and photos; allows users to create profiles and engage with others by posting comments or 'likes'; and, enables users to network with others that hold similar interests or opinions (Obar & Wildman, 2015).

Technology companies such as Google and Facebook have become powerful due to the vast amount of data they holding detailing the internet activity of their billions of users (De Zwart et al., 2014). How information available on the internet is presented to users also has a significant capacity to influence social views and trends. In contrast with traditional mediums, there is a relative lack of central control over content that can facilitate mistruths to be perpetuated.

It has recently been proposed in a number of countries around the world, that social media users must provide evidence of their identity, such as a copy of a passport or drivers licence in order to obtain, or maintain a social media account (Australian Parliament, 2021). The objective of this approach is to address the issue of people using anonymous accounts to harass and abuse online: described as 'technology facilitated abuse', or commit other crimes.[13] In an anonymous online

---

[13] Ibid, Recommendation 30.

environment, vitriolic comments can be widely observed on public social media websites. Online harassment may target individuals or groups on the basis of race, ethnicity, religion or sexual orientation, and is widespread, with recent survey data indicating that one in three have experienced some form of online harassment impacting their health, safety and productivity (Australia Institute, 2019).

There are other issues arising from social media that may also be mitigated with the introduction of identity verification measures. The dissemination of misleading or inaccurate information or theories, commonly referred to as 'fake news', that can rely on automated dissemination using botnets: such as misinformation (conspiracy theories and pseudoscientific therapies) in relation to the COVID-19 pandemic (Naeem, 2020). The efficiency with which social media can disseminate information was highlighted (in association with big data analytics) by the former consultancy firm Cambridge Analytica's online advertising strategies for the Republican Party in the 2016 presidential election campaign. In association with poll results and other intelligence, the firm sought to identify and understand individuals in key electorates, then use social media advertisements specifically targeting their personality and social views to influence their vote (Wong, 2019).[14] These and other developments over recent years, along with the extent to which it is now used around the world, means that social media can significantly impact the lives of individuals and the nature of society. There is an argument that 'social media is too powerful now to be anonymous' and that just as identification and registration is required to drive a car or own a firearm, so it should also be required to operate a social media account (Burns, 2018).

To date, laws requiring compulsory identity verification for social media account holders have not been introduced. They could plausibly deter online harassment and abuse, hate speech and disinformation and enable it to be better investigated and prosecuted. However, there are some potential issues with the approach that should be noted. For example, data security, if identity documents, such as copies of passports and drivers licences, were provided to multinational technology companies such as Google and Facebook, which already have a great deal of personal data about users online and real world (e.g. location metadata) behaviour, they would be a target for organised crime groups, and would increase the level of risk associated with the already detailed and sensitive information that social media companies hold about individuals. There would need to be confidence that this risk could be adequately mitigated before implementation (Druce, 2021).

---

[14] The firm was later dissolved after criticism about the legality of hiring the firm for the presidential campaign in light of prohibitions on the involvement of foreign citizens in United States election campaigns and whether the scale of the activity had compromised the integrity of the election itself. In 2019, Facebook was fined US$5 billion over its management of user data following inquiries into the arrangement.

4.2 Ethical Analysis

In earlier chapters on specific biometrics, namely, fingerprinting, facial recognition technology and DNA, we discussed a number of (often recurring) ethical or moral problems. Central among these was the conflict between individual (including joint (Miller, 2003)) rights to privacy/autonomy/ownership of biometric data, on the one hand, and the collective good of security (Miller, 2010 Ch. 2), on the other hand. Provision of the collective good of security via, for instance, databases of fingerprints, facial images or DNA, was framed as a collective (understood as joint) moral responsibility (Miller, 2006, 2010 Ch. 4). On the other hand since, as we argued, there were moral costs associated with the creation of these databases and, in particular, the infringement of individual rights to privacy and/or autonomy and/or ownership of biometric data, there was a requirement to engage in ethical analysis with a view to accommodating these individual rights in the context of pursuing the collective good of security.

In this chapter, by contrast with earlier chapters, we have described a plethora of interconnected indeed, in many cases, integrated biometric and non-biometric technologies, including databases and associated analytics, smartphone and other applications, encryption and so on. Each of these developments calls for ethical analysis in a piecemeal fashion, but we cannot embark on these analyses in any detail here. For these analyses would take us well beyond our specific focus on biometrics, even if space limitations permitted which they do not. However, we suggest that most of these developments, whether taken singly or in totality, involve a conflict between individual rights and collective goods and, as such, the ethical machinery developed in earlier chapters remains relevant to the required ethical analyses. For instance, the use of metadata by law enforcement and national security, and of smartphone applications for contact tracing in combating COVID 19 can be framed in this manner, or so we have argued elsewhere (Miller & Smith, 2021). Again, the integration of biometric databases (e.g. fingerprint, facial image and DNA databases) with non-biometric databases (e.g. financial or health databases) could greatly facilitate law enforcement and, thereby, increase the collective good of security (Miller, 2010 Ch. 2), but would do so at some (potentially unacceptable) moral cost in terms of infringements, if not violations, of individual rights, as the Snowden revelations (Miller & Walsh, 2016) demonstrated (see the following chapter for more on this issue). Moreover, the existence of these databases is not simply an unalloyed security benefit, since databases give rise to data security concerns in the first instance, and indirectly other wider security concerns, including law enforcement and national security concerns (Miller & Walsh, 2016; Miller & Bossomaier, 2021). For instance, databases can be hacked, and personal and confidential data compromised (including the data of law enforcement or national security agencies). Databases can also be encrypted by malevolent actors for purposes of blackmail i.e. so-called ransomware attacks, e.g. on the National Health Service in the UK. Favoured targets here include hospitals and other organisations whose data is relied upon for health purposes, including to save lives.

Other specific issues with a biometrics aspect, such as encryption and social media touched on above, also implicate privacy and autonomy rights in ways that problematize any easy framing of the ethical issues in terms of individual rights versus collective goods (Miller, 2003, 2010 Ch. 12 Sec. 2). For instance, end-to-end encryption has greatly assisted criminal organisations and thwarted law enforcement, as well as ensuring the privacy of the communications of ordinary law-abiding citizens. Arguably, therefore, citizens do not have a moral right to end-to-end encryption as libertarians are inclined to believe. Again, social media has enabled the proliferation of harmful false hoods (e.g. fake news, and ideology) and thereby demonstrated what should have been obvious, namely, that there is no *unqualified* right to free speech (Miller, 2020). At any rate, social media is in need of regulation, but the ethical issues in this area are very complex and cannot simply be framed in terms of individual rights versus collective goods (albeit this is an important dimension of the moral problem) (Miller & Bossomaier, 2021).

We suggest that in addition to piecemeal analyses of these ethical problems there is a need to take a bird's eye view and consider, in particular, the extent to which these various technologically-based developments have created unacceptable power imbalances between the citizenry on the one hand, and the state on the other (and perhaps, also, between the citizenry and large corporations). The general issue here is that of the potential to undermine fundamental tenets of liberal democracy. We discuss this issue in more detail in the following chapter.

We also suggest that most of these developments, whether taken singly or in totality, involve what is referred to in the literature, and as foreshadowed above, as dual use ethical dilemmas (Miller & Selgelid, 2007; Rappert & Selgelid, 2013; Miller, 2018). We suggest that the notion of dual use ethical dilemmas can usefully frame and elucidate many of the overarching ethical issues that arise from the use in law enforcement and national security contexts of biometrics and, especially, the integration of biometric and non-biometric technologies. This is essentially because although the use of biometrics integrated with non-biometrics can bring great benefits in terms of security it can also impose great moral costs. These moral costs connect the problem of dual use dilemmas to that of concerns about liberal democracy. For, as we will see in the next chapter, the great moral costs in question are dramatically evidenced in the use of these technologies in authoritarian states, such as China, to control the citizenry but also, at least potentially, in those liberal democracies which use these technologies in unacceptable ways or without adequate safeguards. Let us now turn to a more detailed account of dual use dilemmas.

4.2.1 Dual Use Ethical Dilemmas

Dual use technology can be considered a single technology with a dual use or as two (or more) technologies which in combination have a dual use. Thus, research on the transmissibility of a pathogen undertaken in a secure laboratory for the purpose of developing a vaccine might be (potentially) hugely beneficial to humankind.

However, since such research might involve the production of a more transmissible form of the pathogen in question it could also enable a malevolent actor with biological training, such as an 'end-of-the-world' terrorist, to deliberately cause a hugely harmful pandemic (Miller & Selgelid, 2007; Rappert & Selgelid, 2013; Miller, 2018 Ch. 8). This example is an instance of a single type of scientific research having a dual use. Now consider facial recognition technology integrated with CCTV camera technology to enable the tracking of individuals. This integrated combination of technologies is dual use in that it could be used by police only to track persons guilty (or, at least, reasonably suspected of being guilty) of serious crimes (Miller & Gordon, 2014) i.e. it is used only for necessary and legitimate law enforcement; or it could be used to monitor ordinary citizens' behaviour in order to ensure their compliance with the human rights-violating dictates of an authoritarian government.

Our main focus in this chapter is with dual use ethical dilemmas arising from the integration of biometric and non-biometric technologies i.e. with biometric and non-biometric technologies taken in combination. Our reason for doing so is that dual use ethical dilemmas in biometrics arise in their most acute form when biometrics are integrated with non-biometric technologies, such as facial recognition technology with CCTV camera technology, or biometric databases integrated with non-biometric databases and associated analytics, such as facial image databases of known persons (e.g. derived from passport photos) integrated with phone metadata databases, social security databases, social media data mined from social media sites etc. potentially enabling the development of profiles of particular individuals suspected of crimes but also potentially enabling authoritarian states to monitor and suppress their populations; or, in the case of private companies, to develop customer profiles for the potential purpose of better meeting their needs but also potentially enabling large-scale manipulation of customers to enhance the profits of companies (Zuboff, 2019). Another general area of concern here might be the interlinking not only of biometric and non-biometric databases and use of associated analytics, such as data mining or machine learning techniques (Miller & Bossomaier, 2021), but also the interlinking of government and private sector held databases (of which more below).

The problem of dual-use ethical dilemmas in relation to powerful, new and emerging technologies, including biometrics integrated with non-biometrics, arises because such technologies have the potential to be used for great harm as well as for great good (See e.g. Miller & Selgelid, 2007; Rappert & Selgelid, 2013; Meier & Hunger, 2014; Miller, 2018). On the one hand, such technologies can contribute greatly to individual and collective well-being. Consider, for example, nuclear technology that enables the generation of low cost electricity in populations without obvious alternative energy sources. So, as mentioned above, nuclear technology is a good thing. On the other hand, these same technologies can be extremely harmful to individuals and collectives. Consider, for example, the atomic bombs dropped on Hiroshima and Nagasaki. So it seems that some powerful technologies or, at least, some uses of some powerful technologies, are a bad thing and, therefore, knowledge of these technologies is a bad thing and ignorance a good thing. Accordingly, the question arises as to whether we ought to limit the development of these

4.2 Ethical Analysis

technologies or, more likely, restrict the uses of these technologies and, in particular, the proliferation of these technologies and perhaps dissemination of the knowledge how to develop them (assuming this is possible).

By definition, dual use technologies are potentially harmful as well as beneficial, and therefore, there is a need to limit these technologies, or their uses, in a manner that decreases the risk of harm while preserving the benefits. In relation to the potential for harm, governments, regulators, scientists, designers and manufacturers technology and, in the cases of interest to us, law enforcement and national security agencies who use the technology, have a moral responsibility and, specifically a collective or joint moral responsibility. This is so, even if there is not at present a legal responsibility, to cooperate in order to avert or, at least, minimise the risks. Dual use research and technology is a matter of *collective moral responsibility* to avert or minimise harm (Miller, 2018 Ch. 4). But how does collective responsibility figure in the various scientific, technological and institutional contexts in question? More specifically, should some dual use research and technologies be impermissible or, if not, should certain uses of these technologies be curtailed? For instance, in some jurisdiction in US and in the EU, certain uses of facial recognition technology have been banned. More generally, what institutional arrangements, e.g. regulations, ought to be put in place in relation to dual use biometric technologies and uses thereof, specifically in the context of this work by security agencies?

"Dual use" refers to scientific research or technology that can be used for both beneficial/good and harmful/bad purposes (See e.g. Miller & Selgelid, 2007; Miller, 2013, 2018; Meier & Hunger, 2014; Tucker, 2012). However, this general sense of dual use is too broad since it has the effect that almost everything could count as dual use. For instance, machetes are used for farming, but they were also used in the Rwandan genocide in 1994 as tools of murder. So we require a narrower notion of dual use. Most of the current debate has focused on research and technologies with implications not simply for weapons but for weapons of mass destruction (WMDs), in particular – i.e., where the harmful consequences of malevolent use would be on an extremely large scale (Miller, 2018). That said, defining dual use simply in terms of WMDs yields too narrow a notion given, for instance, the possibility of creating de novo new pathogens which are both highly virulent and highly transmissible (NSABB, 2015; Selgelid, 2016). Moreover, the biometric technologies of interest to us in this work do not have any obvious implications for WMDs, yet they are potentially able to cause serious harms on a very large scale in the hands, for instance, of authoritarian governments. Accordingly, let us try to get a better fix on a serviceable notion of dual use by setting out a number of different preliminary definitions of dual use familiar in the literature and doing so on the assumption that any definition will involve a degree of stipulation (Miller & Selgelid, 2007; Miller, 2018 Ch. 1).

Research or technology is dual use if it can be used for both:

1. Military and civilian (i.e. non-military) purposes; or
2. Beneficial and harmful purposes – where the harmful purposes are to be realised by means of WMDs; or

3. Beneficial and harmful purposes – where either the harmful purposes involve the use of weapons as means, and usually WMDs in particular, or the large-scale harm aimed at does not necessarily involve weapons or weaponisation[15].

We favour the third definition of "dual use" since some dual use research, such as gain-of-function research in the biological sciences, or research in biometrics leading to the increasing sophistication of facial recognition technology or the integration of biometric and non-biometric databases (and use of associated data analytics), need not involve an explicit process of weaponisation or a military purpose. Moreover, whereas biometrics can assist in the realisation of military purposes, e.g. facial recognition technology used on predator drones to identify nominated human targets to be killed: facial recognition technology is not a weapon per se.

Dual-use refers to two conceptually distinct groups of actors[16]: (i) those who initially undertake the research and/or develop the technology (let us refer to these as original researchers/developers); and (ii) those who use the results of the work of these original researchers/developers, e.g. security agencies. In the case of dual use technologies, the original researchers/developers presumably designed the technology with the intention that it be used for beneficial purposes, even if they were aware that it could also be used for harmful purposes. The general point being that their intention was not that it be exclusively or predominantly used for harmful purposes, as in the case of weapons technology. That said, dual use technologies are, to reiterate, technologies that could be used for harmful purposes and it is certainly possible that dual use technologies were designed to be used for both beneficial as well as harmful purposes.

In relation to the term, "use", we can distinguish: (i) actually or potentially used in accordance with the purpose for which it was designed (design-purpose); (ii) actually or potentially used for some purpose other than that for which it was specifically designed; (iii) actually or potentially used for a benevolent and, therefore let us assume , morally good purpose; (iv) actually or potentially used for a malevolent and, therefore, morally bad purpose.[17] Dual-use dilemmas typically involve: (A) original researchers/developers undertaking scientific research or developing technology for a good purpose – the design-purpose is good; and (B) malevolent secondary (actual or potential) users – the research is to be used to cause great harm. This is consistent with their being some other group of original researchers who had a malevolent design-purpose. However, on our definition of dual use there needs to

---

[15] There is a distinction between an object which is a weapon merely because used as one, e.g. a brick used to hit someone on the head, and a weapon which was designed as such from material which is not in itself useable as a weapon and, therefore, needs to go through a process of weaponisation, e.g. a biological agent used in a bioweapon.

[16] Two things can be conceptually distinct even if under some description they are the same thing. Thus being married is conceptually distinct from being a scientist. However, Jones can be a married scientist. Similarly, the original researcher could also be the secondary user, notwithstanding that original researcher and secondary user are distinct concepts.

[17] We are assuming that in the final analysis the dual use dilemma is a moral dilemma and, therefore, the harms and benefits in question are morally significant (either directly or indirectly).

be a group of original researchers who have a good purpose (even if they designed the technology is a manner that enable it also to be used for a bad purpose). This good purpose is either a good design-purpose or a morally neutral design-purpose which is a means to some further good purpose that they have.

Consider facial recognition technology. It was designed, obviously, to enable people to be identified by use of facial images. Accordingly, in the hands of appropriately regulated law enforcement agencies in a liberal democratic state facial recognition technology, let us assume, would be used to identify criminals and reduce crime (especially, as we saw above, if integrated with other technologies, such as CCTV camera technology and/or integrated biometric and non-biometric databases, e.g. of passport photos, phone metadata). However, in the hands of politically-driven security agencies in an authoritarian state it may well be used to identify people who are innocent of any crime other than standing up for their human rights. Thus, facial recognition technology, especially taken in conjunction integrated non-biometric (and other biometric) technologies is an instance of dual use technology. Another non-biometric example of dual use technology is encryption – this was designed to protect privacy and confidentiality and, other things being equal, this is a good thing. However, criminals use encryption in ransomware attacks to blackmail organisations to pay them money on pain of not being able to retrieve their data which, in the case of hospitals, may threaten life itself (Miller, 2018 Ch. 7).

In relation to the *avoidable*[18] *outcomes* of the scientific research or technology, we can distinguish: (i) intended outcomes; (ii) unintended but foreseen outcomes; (iii) unforeseen (but foreseeable) outcomes; and (iv) unforeseeable outcomes (Miller, 2018 Ch. 1). An example of an unintended outcome is the spread of radiotoxic material into the environment from a damaged nuclear reactor resulting from a tsunami, as happened in Fukushima, Japan in 2011. However, such accidents are not obviously instances of the dual-use dilemma. For something to be an instance of a dual-use dilemma, both outcomes (the two horns of the dual-use dilemma) need to be (actually or potentially) intended (or at least foreseen or foreseeable) by someone; there needs to be two sets of (actual or potential) *users*. Naturally, an outcome might be unintended and unforeseen (even unforeseeable) by the original researcher or technologist but, nevertheless, intended by the user. Thus, scientists who develop the process of nuclear fission to be used for power generation might not intend or foresee that the same process might be used to build atomic bombs. Again, those who developed facial recognition technology *might* not have intended or foreseen that it might be used by authoritarian governments to assist in the repression of their populations. On the other hand, perhaps this was a foreseeable outcome, if not a foreseen one. Again, the establishment of biometric databases integrated with non-biometric databases (and associated analytics) may well have been driven in many instances by a desire to enhance legitimate law enforcement purposes or to enhance

---

[18] We are assuming that the relevant outcomes of dual use research are avoidable even if only by refraining from conducting the research. We are further assuming that the scientists in question could have avoided conducting the research. This raises the question of scientists operating in authoritarian states who are coerced into conducting certain research.

health outcomes for the population at large. However, these developments, as already mentioned, have the potential for great harm in the hands of authoritarian states.

Many, if not most, so-called dual use dilemmas are not really dilemmas in the narrow sense of being situations involving two options which are equally morally problematic. In the first place, the dilemmas in question could be tri-lemmas; indeed, there could be four or five or some very large number of options all of which are equally morally problematic. In the second place, the options are not generally *equally* morally problematic. Thus refusing to introduce facial recognition technology or population wide DNA databases might render legitimate law enforcement less effective but introducing either of these might lead to significant violations of citizens' autonomy. Certainly, there are moral considerations for and against each of the options, however it may well be that, all things considered, one of the options is morally preferable to the others and that this is relatively obvious to any rational, morally sensitive person. The point is rather that there are at least some significant moral costs associated with each of the available options. Moreover, there is always the possibility of designing these technologies and the institutional arrangements in which they are embedded in a manner that greatly reducing the potential harms while preserving most of the benefits (van den Hoven et al., 2017). Accountability systems are a way of achieving this in some cases, limiting access to these technologies in other cases (Miller, 2018).

As already noted many, if not most, scientific discoveries and, especially, new technologies, have dual use potential in the trivial sense that they could be used by someone for some malevolent purpose. Indeed, any newly designed object, such as the first baseball bat, has dual use potential in this trivial sense. After all, baseball bats can be used to hit people over the head, as well as for the enjoyment of playing baseball. However, it is implicit in the use of the term "dual use" in play in the academic literature that the potential harm in question is of a very great magnitude and it is caused by a technology (rather than merely a rudimentarily fashioned physical object).

Note that accidents involving science and technology, even accidents on a very large scale, such as the Union Carbide Bhopal chemical disaster and the Chernobyl and Fukushima nuclear disasters, are not *necessarily* dual use in our sense since there is no secondary evil user. More generally, questions of security should be conceptually demarcated from questions of safety.

Nevertheless, such disasters might be dual use if they were predictable. Here two points need to be kept in mind. Firstly, if it is more or less predictable that there will be a *morally culpable large-scale harm-causing* secondary user of the science and technology in question then it may be dual use, notwithstanding that this secondary user did not *intend* to do evil. Perhaps there is gross negligence with respect to safety on the part of a secondary user (who might in fact also be the original researcher) leading to massive loss of life and this was foreseen (or, at least, reasonably foreseeable) by the original researchers. Accordingly, the line between safety and security is in practice blurred; it is blurred at the point at which there is culpable negligence. Culpable negligence is both a safety and a security issue; hence by our lights dual use issues while primarily matters of security are also to some extent matters of safety. Once again there is an element of stipulation here. However, we are seeking a concept of dual use that does not embrace unforeseeable accidents; surely an unforeseeable accident is not a *use* since it is not an *act* per se but rather an event. The notion of culpability serves our purpose here since, arguably, those who are culpably negligent have committed (in some sense) *acts* of omission. Secondly, the original research which enabled the construction of such industrial plants might be dual use. Thus the process of nuclear fission which has as a by-product highly radioactive fissile material may well be dual use, given the known risk of large-scale harm to humankind posed by such material. Again, health data bases, including genomic data, may be hugely beneficial in part because relied upon by hospitals but if data security is not maintained and, for instance, a ransomware attack renders this data unusable threatening lives, then the harm caused can also be on a very large scale (Miller & Bossomaier, 2021).

Dual use technologies are inherently morally problematic since they are, by definition, technologies that can confer great benefits but also cause (in the wrong hands) great harm. Biometric technologies are no exception. However, the harms potentially caused by biometric technologies are perhaps more insidious that those of some other dual use technologies, e.g. nuclear technology, since biometric technologies do not lend themselves directly to weaponization and, in particular, to being used as WMDs (other than in a figurative sense). This is because although biometric technology enables malevolent actors to cause great harm, it is an essentially epistemic (or knowledge-focussed) technology, e.g. it consists in epistemic action rather than kinetic action (see e.g. Henschke, 2017 Ch. 9; Miller, 2021). Naturally, knowledge enables kinetic action, e.g. identifying someone as a criminal enables his or her arrest. However, identification of an individual via fingerprints, facial images or DNA, even it is a violation of, for instance, their right to privacy, does not necessarily in and of itself cause harm; rather it enables harm to be caused by further kinetic actions.

4.3 Conclusion

The rise of data analytics, smartphones, metadata, social media and artificial intelligence over the past decade has resulted in a broader range of data and identification techniques about individuals to become available, which can by analysed and exploited for a range of purposes. These new forms of data are entwined with, and in some cases facilitated by biometric identification, to constitute a complex contemporary digital identity. Biometric security is likely to play a key role in improving cybersecurity, presently a significant social issue, as well as in relation to online safety, potentially having a role in increasing regulation to address online anonymity. As we have discussed, biometrics – especially when integrated with non-biometric technologies – can be used for beneficial purposes, such as increasing security on devices, identifying criminals or, more generally, greatly increasing the effectiveness of law enforcement agencies. However, they can also be used for a harmful purpose, such as enabling an authoritarian government to surveil a population. We suggest that law reform arguments in relation to the use of these technologies and associated data can be usefully elucidated through being framed as dual use ethical dilemmas. Appropriate laws should enable biometric identification technologies to be used in ways that benefit society, such as increasing security and efficiency, but regulate and restrict use, so that the potential for privacy violation and other harms are limited as far as possible. Although the use of biometrics can bring great benefits in terms of security, they can also impose great moral costs that raise concerns about liberal democracy in the absence of adequate safeguards, as will be explored further in the final chapter.

References

Australian Criminal Intelligence Commission, Biometric and forensic services. (2021). https://www.acic.gov.au/services/biometric-and-forensic-services

Australia Institute. (2019). *Online harassment and cyberhate costs Australians $3.7b*. https://australiainstitute.org.au/post/online-harassment-and-cyberhate-costs-australians-3-7b/

Australian National University. (2019). *Incident report into the ANU data breach*. https://www.anu.edu.au/news/all-news/data-breach

Australian Parliament. (2021). *Inquiry into family, domestic and sexual violence*. House Standing Committee on Social Policy and Legal Affairs.

Bogle, A. (2020, 27 April). Will the government's coronavirus app COVIDSafe keep your data secure? Here's what the experts say. *Australian Broadcasting Corporation News*.

Brayne, S. (2017). Big data surveillance: The case of policing. *American Sociological Review, 82*, 977–1008.

Burns, W. (2018, 2 February). Is it time to require identity verification for everyone using social media? *Forbes*. https://www.forbes.com/sites/willburns/2018/02/22/is-it-time-to-require-identity-verification-for-everyone-using-social-media/?sh=6bb464528683

De Zwart, M., Humphreys, S., & Van Dissel, B. (2014). Surveillance, big data and democracy: Lessons for Australia from the US and UK. *University of New South Wales Law Journal, 37*, 713–747.

Dencik, L., & Cable, J. (2017). The advent of surveillance realism: Public opinion and activist responses to the Snowden leaks. *International Journal of Communication, 11*, 763–765.

Druce, A. (2021, 2 April). It's a long bow': Social media ID push dubbed ineffective, a privacy risk. *Sydney Morning Herald*. https://www.smh.com.au/politics/federal/it-s-a-long-bow-social-media-id-push-dubbed-a-privacy-risk-20210402-p57g7d.html

Federal Bureau of Investigation. (2021). *Next Generation Identification*. https://www.fbi.gov/services/cjis/fingerprintsand-other-biometrics/ngi

Halbfinger, D., Kershner, I., & Bergman, R. (2020, 16 March). To track coronavirus, Israel moves to tap secret trove of cellphone data. *New York Times*. https://www.nytimes.com/2020/03/16/world/middleeast/israel-coronavirus-cellphone-tracking.html

Henschke, A. (2017). *Ethics in an age of surveillance: Virtual identities and personal information*. Cambridge University Press.

Kaye, J., et al. (2015). Dynamic consent: A patient interface for twenty-first century research networks. *European Journal of Human Genetics, 23*, 141–146.

References

Koper, C., Lum, C., & Willis, J. (2014). Optimizing the use of technology in policing: Results and implications from a multi-site study of the social, organizational, and behavioural aspects of implementing police technologies. *Policing, 8*(2), 212–221.

Meier, O., & Hunger, I. (2014). *Between control and cooperation: Dual-use, technology transfers and the non-proliferation of weapons of mass destruction*. Deutsche Stiftung Friedensforschung.

Miller, S. (2003). Institutions, collective goods and individual rights. *Protosociology, 18*, 184–207.

Miller, S. (2006). Collective moral responsibility: An individualist account. *Midwest Studies in Philosophy, XXX*, 176–193.

Miller, S. (2018). *Dual use science and technology, ethics and weapons of mass*. Springer.

Miller, S. (2020). Freedom of political communication, propaganda and the role of epistemic institutions. In M. Christen, B. Gordjin, & M. Loi (Eds.), *Ethics of cybersecurity*. Springer.

Miller, S. (2021). Rethinking the just intelligence theory of national security intelligence collection and analysis: Principles of discrimination, necessity, proportionality and reciprocity. *Social Epistemology, 35*.

Miller, S., & Bossomaier, T. (2021). *Ethics and cybersecurity*. Oxford University Press.

Miller, S., & Gordon, I. (2014). *Investigative ethics: Ethics for police detectives and criminal investigators*. Blackwell.

Miller, S., & Selgelid, M. (2007). Ethical and philosophical consideration of the dual use dilemma in the biological sciences. *Science and Engineering Ethics, 13*, 523–580.

Miller, S., & Smith, M. (2021). Ethics, public health and technology responses to COVID-19. *Bioethics, 35*.

Miller, S., & Walsh, P. (2016). NSA, Snowden and the ethics and accountability of intelligence gathering. In J. Galliott & J. Reed (Eds.), *Ethics and the future of spying: Technology, intelligence collection and national security* (pp. 193–204). Routledge.

Murphy, J. (2014). *Access to and retention of internet 'metadata'*. Australian Parliamentary Library.

Naeem, S. B. (2020). An exploration of how fake news is taking over social media and putting public health at risk. *Health information and libraries journal, 11*, 1–7.

Nakashima, E., & Albergotti, R. (2021, 14 April). The FBI wanted to unlock the San Bernardino shooter's iPhone. It turned to a little-known Australian firm. *The Washington Post*. https://www.washingtonpost.com/technology/2021/04/14/azimuth-san-bernardino-apple-iphone-fbi/

National Science Advisory Board for Biosecurity (NSABB). (2015). *Framework for conducting risk benefit assessments of gain-of-function research*.

Obar, J., & Wildman, S. (2015). Social media definition and the governance challenge: An introduction to the special issue. *Telecommunications Policy, 39*, 745–750.

Pannett, R., & Birnbaum, M. (2021, 9 June). FBI-controlled anom app ensnares scores of alleged criminals in global police sting. *Washington Post*. https://www.washingtonpost.com/world/2021/06/08/fbi-app-arrests-australia-crime/

Pollack, M. (2019). Taking data. *University of Chicago Law Review, 86*, 77–141.

Pramanik, M., et al. (2017). Big data analytics for security and criminal investigations. *WIREs Data Mining Knowledge Discovery, 7*, 1–19.

Rappert, B., & Selgelid, M. (Eds.). (2013). *On the dual uses of science and ethics: Principles, practices and prospects*. ANU Press.

Ratcliffe, J. H. (2008). Intelligence-led policing. In Wortley, R., & Mazerolle, L. (Eds.), *Chapter 14 of Environmental Criminology and Crime Analysis* (pp. 263–282). Willan Publishing.

Redrup, Y. (2019, 23 July). Experts demand increased transparency in metadata surveillance laws. *Australian Financial Review*.

Sarre, R. (2017). Metadata retention as a means of combatting terrorism and organised crime: A perspective from Australia. *Asian Journal of Criminology, 12*, 167–179.

Selgelid, M. (2016). Gain of function research: Ethical analysis. *Science and Engineering Ethics, 22*, 923–964.

Servick, K. (2020, 21 May). COVID-19 contact tracing apps are coming to a phone near you. How will we know whether they work? *Science*. https://www.sciencemag.org/news/2020/05/countries-around-world-are-rolling-out-contact-tracing-apps-contain-coronavirus-how

Sheng, C., & Zijia, H. (2020, 18 July). Is China's 'health code' here to stay? *The Diplomat*.
Smith, M., & Heath Jeffery, R. (2020). Addressing the challenges of artificial intelligence in medicine. *Internal Medicine Journal, 50*, 1278–1281.
Smith, M., & Urbas, G. (2021). *Technology law*. Cambridge University Press.
Tan, W., et al. (2013). Social-network-sourced big data analytics. *IEEE Internet Computing, 17*, 62–69.
The Guardian. (2020, 16 June). *Norway suspends virus-tracing app due to privacy concerns*. https://www.theguardian.com/world/2020/jun/15/norway-suspends-virus-tracing-app-due-to-privacy-concerns
Tucker, J. (Ed.). (2012). *Innovation, dual use, and security*. MIT Press.
van den Hoven, J., Miller, S., & Pogge, T. (2017). *Designing in ethics*. Cambridge University Press.
Walsh, P., & Miller, S. (2016). Rethinking 'five eyes' security intelligence collection policies and practice post Snowden. *Intelligence & National Security, 31*, 345–368.
Wang, M. (2020, 1 April). China: Fighting COVID-19 with automated tyranny. *The Diplomat*.
Williams, M. (2003). Words, images, enemies: Securitization and international politics. *International Studies Quarterly, 47*, 511–531.
Wong, J. (2019, 18 March). The Cambridge Analytica scandal changed the world: But it didn't change Facebook. *The Guardian*. https://www.theguardian.com/technology/2019/mar/17/the-cambridge-analytica-scandal-changed-the-world-but-it-didnt-change-facebook
World Health Organisation. (2020). *Coronavirus disease situation reports*. https://www.who.int/emergencies/diseases/novel-coronavirus-2019/situation-reports
Zuboff, S. (2019). *The age of surveillance capitalism*. Profile Books.

Open Access This chapter is licensed under the terms of the Creative Commons Attribution 4.0 International License (http://creativecommons.org/licenses/by/4.0/), which permits use, sharing, adaptation, distribution and reproduction in any medium or format, as long as you give appropriate credit to the original author(s) and the source, provide a link to the Creative Commons license and indicate if changes were made.

The images or other third party material in this chapter are included in the chapter's Creative Commons license, unless indicated otherwise in a credit line to the material. If material is not included in the chapter's Creative Commons license and your intended use is not permitted by statutory regulation or exceeds the permitted use, you will need to obtain permission directly from the copyright holder.

Chapter 5
The Future of Biometrics and Liberal Democracy

Abstract The first part of this chapter considers future biometrics, with a focus on second generation biometrics that measure physiological patterns. The second discusses the potential biometric future – how the use of biometrics, data and algorithms more broadly, could be used by governments to regulate social and economic interactions. This discussion will draw on the development of credit systems, from those used in commercial online platforms to rate the performance of providers and users, to the more integrated and all-encompassing social credit system (SCS) implemented in China, as an example of a potential future development in liberal democratic countries. Finally, we discuss the key features of liberal democratic theory and how biometric and related technological developments may change governance in western democracies. While we briefly mention some relevant developments in the private sector, our main focus will be on the relationship between liberal democratic governments and their security agencies, on the one hand, and their citizenry, on the other. We describe in general terms how liberal democracies might respond to these new technologies in a manner that preserves their benefits without unduly compromising established liberal democratic institutions, principles and values. Accordingly, we seek to offer a response to some of the dual use ethical dilemmas posed by biometrics, albeit in general terms.

Keywords Biometric identification · Future biometrics · Governance · Digital identity · Social credit system (SCS) · Liberal democracy

5.1 Future Biometrics

There are a range of new biometrics being developed and implemented that provide insights into how biometric technology may influence society in the future. The main biometric identification techniques considered throughout this book – fingerprint, DNA and facial image identification – are examples of first generation biometrics, derived from physical traits. Second generation biometrics, also referred to as behavioural biometrics, measure individual patterns of physiological processes or learned behaviour, rather than physical traits (Smith et al., 2018). These biometrics are less stable and accurate than first generation biometrics and for that reason are not usually used individually, and have not been widely adopted. Examples include cardiac activity (patterns of heart activity), cognitive biometrics (patterns of brain activity) and gait (pattern of walking). Over time, they are likely to have their own specialised applications, and a role in combination with first generation biometrics to increase accuracy. For example, when integrating facial recognition with CCTV footage to identify individuals in a crowd, distance and lighting conditions affect its accuracy – this can be mitigated through the addition of gait analysis. In relation to access to a computer, fingerprint biometrics could be used as an initial password, and keystroke dynamics to monitor that the same individual is continuing to use the device over time. Cognitive biometrics could be used as a second line biometric in a highly secure environment where it is possible that a fingerprint, or other initial method of access, has been replicated (Smith et al., 2018).

The most recently reported second generation biometric is the remote detection of individual cardiac patterns. The United States military has reportedly developed an infrared laser biometric scanner that can detect unique cardiac signatures, through a person's clothes, from hundreds of meters away, and possibly at even further distances. The technique is described as cardiac laser vibrometry and detects surface movements created by a person's unique heartbeat pattern (Smith et al., 2018). One of the key advantages of the technique is that it provides more accurate results than facial recognition, the other biometric application that can be administered from a distance, and is not affected by factors such as light conditions and headwear (Hambling, 2019). The technology could also be used in the private sector as an alternative to fingerprint identification in the future.

A similar technique which has been established for some time, although cannot be administered at a distance, is cognitive biometric identification. This is based on the measurement of electrical signals that are generated in the brain as a result of an individual's thought processes (Revett et al., 2010). These electrical signals generated by neural activity are representative of individuals' mental states and can be measured by brain-computer interfaces known as electroencephalograms (EEG) (Jolfaei et al., 2013). The measurement of cognitive biometrics is a more invasive process that requires electrodes be placed on the subject's scalp – although a more discrete version may become available as the technology develops. It has been demonstrated that electrical signals in the brain are associated with specific stimuli, and that simply thinking of a specific object or password will create a corresponding electrical pattern that is sufficient for authentication via EEG (Armstrong et al., 2015). However, the technique currently has a lower accuracy than other methods, reportedly ranging from 82% to 97% (Bajwa & Dantu, 2016). Another limitation is the invasive process and high cost of the equipment. While technology generally becomes smaller and cheaper over time, cognitive biometrics are unlikely to be used as widely as the main forms of biometrics that have been discussed.

Another important second generation for of biometric identification is gait recognition. This measures the pattern of motion made by an individual's limbs when they walk (Goffredo et al., 2010). It requires an initial setup stage, to establish an individual's gait. A video recording is converted into a representative silhouette and data, such as an individuals' height, limb length and torso shape is recorded (Indumathi & Pushparani, 2016). Environmental conditions such as lighting, distance from the camera, and the type of clothing worn by the subject, can affect its use. It has an accuracy rate of approximately 90%, and as discussed, its main application is in conjunction with facial recognition, as it can be operated from a distance, doesn't require as high resolution images, and can function when the subject's face is obscured (Chaurasia et al., 2015).

The final developing form of biometric identification we will consider is keystroke dynamics. This uses an individual's typing characteristics and patterns, such as key press duration, for identification purposes. It is less reliable than physical biometrics due to the variability in behaviour, but its reliability is related to the length of text typed, (e.g., it would have limited application for short passwords) (Rudrapal et al., 2014). The use of keystroke dynamics could increase in the future as part of dual factor authentication in online environments, however broader adoption will be dependent on the availability keyboards, keypads and smartphone screens with pressure sensors that can be integrated with the technology (Ngugi et al., 2012).

Continued technology advancement will lead to a range of more advanced new biometrics being developed in the future; and existing biometrics will become increasing sophisticated and applied in new ways. However, it is the coordinated use of biometrics and big data by governments and corporations that will have the biggest impact on society in the future. In the absence of public debate and law reform to regulate their use, there is potential for these to be used in a way that alters the nature of liberal democracies as they exist today – this will be the focus of the remainder of the chapter.

5.2 Biometric Futures

5.2.1 Social Credit Systems

Developments taking place today in China provide a picture of the direction liberal democracies may shift in the decades ahead as biometric databases and other datasets become more widely available and are used more extensively. The SCS has been developing over the past 20 years and is continuing to advance towards a future society where each citizen is allocated a score representing their honesty and integrity (Sıthigh & Siems, 2019). That score will dictate their lifestyle and access to government and commercial services, including whether a bank will give them a credit card or loan; whether they can travel on public transport; and the schools their children can attend. While this concept is used in specific contexts in liberal democracies, such as in credit scores calculated by lenders, or to rate the integrity of sellers and buyers in online marketplaces, these are not as far reaching or comprehensive as the SCS. Instead of being limited to behaviour in a specific domain, such as meeting financial obligations, or honouring contracts entered into when buying or selling goods, the fully developed SCS will be all-encompassing in dictating personal actions and behaviours (Sıthigh & Siems, 2019).

The impact of the SCS on individuals becomes more significant and divergent from western versions when used for political purposes in an authoritarian state – such as making judgments about an individual's character, and identifying dissidents or those opposed to certain policies of the Chinese Communist Party, and enforcing consequences against individuals that don't comply. To achieve this end, biometric identification, integrating facial recognition with an extensive public CCTV network, DNA identification, and phone metadata; as well as and big data analytics using sources such as financial and medical records, provide the basis for establishing complete surveillance of a population. As technologies like facial recognition and artificial intelligence become even more widely used, the risk increases that personal data and identity will facilitate a more extensive authoritarian algorithmic governance model (Danaher et al., 2017).

The State Council of the People's Republic of China published a planning outline for the construction of a social credit system in 2014. This publication sets out their rationale for implementing the SCS, with the official goal being the 'construction of sincerity in government affairs, commercial sincerity, social sincerity, and judicial credibility', through greater transparency in government policy making (SCPRC, 2014). A variety of social issues relating to trust that the SCS seeks to address, include fraud, counterfeit goods, tax evasion and food contamination. The Chinese government asserts that moving to a credit-based economy reduces transaction and government intervention in the market, while increasing the country's competitiveness in the global economy. The Chinese government describes three aspects of the SCS. First, the creation of a large interconnected dataset, drawing on the holdings of government and non-government entities, creating: 'Interconnection and interactivity of…credit information systems and…networks that cover all information subjects, all credit information categories, and all regions nationwide' (SCPRC, 2014). This includes data from individuals, businesses, NGOs and government agencies. Second, the application of that data to encourage individuals and organisations to be more trustworthy by preventing those that commit transgressions from accessing services. This operates in the same way that committing traffic offences can lead to a loss of licence; a criminal record can limit employment prospects; or a poor credit rating can make it difficult to obtain a loan from a bank. While some aspects are similar to existing measures in liberal democracies, the SCS is more extensive, implementing automated law enforcement and economic regulation across all aspects of society. Individuals rated as untrustworthy in one aspect of their life may not be able to access services, such as obtaining tickets for flights or high speed rail travel, booking hotel rooms, or accessing the internet. Aside from the inherent rights violations, notably violations of privacy and autonomy, involved in this degree of state interference in the lives of individual citizens, it can also lead to what has been described as a form of informational injustice (van den Hoven, 2008), where information provided in one context can change its meaning when used in another way that leads to disadvantage or discrimination for an individual.

The final aspect is the publication of data to warn members of the public about transacting with untrustworthy individuals and shaming them to alter their behaviour. While details of criminal trials are published in the media in most countries around the world, some Chinese cities have been shaming offenders of minor crimes, such as jaywalking – identifying them using facial recognition technology and posting their image on large public video screens. It has been reported that in cities such as Shenzhen, Jinan and Fuzhou, facial recognition technology has been used to identify offenders who have committed minor crimes such as jaywalking or taking toilet paper from public toilets, and publish their names and pictures on billboards or in the media. Galič et al. (2017) relevantly describes the SCS as '…a tool for assimilating biopower into digital systems' monitoring the faces and movements of bodies in physical spaces as digital representations of individuals.

Many of these measures are extensions or adapted forms of approaches undertaken around the world, and there could be efficiencies and benefits of applying data and technologies such as biometrics to these ends: 'A well-governed SCS could bring transparency, oversee those in power, regulate the economy with less direct government intervention, and encourage people to treat each other more fairly, as the government maintains' (Wong & Dobson, 2019, p. 224). However, there are more concerning aspects that have already begun to be implemented, such as those relating to free speech. Chinese social media sites that allow users to post online commentary are required to maintain lists of those that make statements considered illegal, which can then be integrated in the broader SCS:

> …based on China's record of regulating political speech and other activities, there is no doubt that it could also be abused for social control, prying into every aspect of Chinese citizens' lives and automatically punishing those who don't toe the party line. As in the West, which is awakening to uses and abuses of privately collected data, China's experiment raises moral and economic questions about collection and use of data, which are at the core of the most promising innovations and critical governance challenges worldwide (Chorzempa et al., 2018).

There are parallels between the SCS and the rating systems used in online platforms such as Uber or Airbnb, and the ratings or likes on social media platforms such as Facebook and Instagram (Dahlberg, 2015; Sıthigh & Siems, 2019). These systems quantify individual reputations – those who have higher ratings promoted by the platforms algorithms – and great volumes of data are collected about users and applied for advertising purposes. However, in noting the parallels here, there is a key difference between the SCS which is established and implemented to achieve a political objective, and the use of rating systems in online platforms such as Uber, which are implemented to ensure their platform runs effectively– ultimately a commercial objective. While social media images, posts or metadata is of interest to the governments, particularly in the context of a law enforcement investigation to identify where a person of interest has been, what they have done, or who they have communicated with; the fact that an individual is a courteous Uber driver or passenger, or guest of an Airbnb, is of little interest to government.

On the other hand, there are some parallels between SCS, governments and security agencies in liberal democracies and corporations in respect of control of personal data including, potentially biometric data. As we have seen, liberal democratic governments and their security agencies have established significant such databases (and employed associated analytics). However, technology corporations, such as Facebook and Google, have adopted a business model according to which individuals provide their personal data in return for 'free' use of internet services. technology corporations. These corporations have been collecting very large amounts of data from their users, e.g. those who conduct searches on Google and those who communicate with their friends on Facebook, and doing so without their knowledge, let alone consent or, at the very least, without their consent until the recent enactment of the European Union's General Data Protection Regulation 2016/679 (GDPR) (although the GDPR only covers the EU and those who interact with the EU). Importantly, these corporations continue to collect very large amounts of data from their users without the *strong* consent of these users (see Chap. 1). Accordingly, this bulk data (or, at least a good deal of it, depending on which particular kind(s) and extent of data, is in question) has been collected in violation of the privacy/data control rights of users of Google and Facebook services. Moreover, data analytics, e.g. machine learning, has been deployed to structure this data in a manner suitable for commercial purposes, notably advertising purposes, e.g. profiles of customers are developed to enable better targeted and, therefore, more efficient and effective, advertisements. The corporations using this data for commercial purposes include not only the corporations who originally collected the data, but also the myriad of other corporations who, as it turns out, they on-sell the data to. Further, according to Zuboff (2019), these commercial activities are not simply to be understood as violations of privacy/data control rights or, as she puts it, the extraction of 'behavioral surplus'. For the quantum of data in question, and the power of the data analytics used, is such as to enable the creation of 'predictive products'. For instance, a bank might construct a new financial product based on far more accurate profiles of bank customers than their use of the bank's existing products. Thus: 'one recent study used the mobility data generated by 100,000 bank customers' cell phones over a one-year period to predict with very high accuracy their likely demand for a given loan product.'[1] Given this predictive ability and the ability to use manipulative techniques, e.g. subliminal advertising and the use of so-called 'nudges' (Thaler & Sunstein, 2009), the possibility of 'behavioral modification' emerges, although Zuboff herself emphasizes the predictive ability as opposed to what we take to be the conceptually separable manipulative techniques. Of course, the power of manipulative techniques is enormously enhanced by predictive ability. At any rate, important questions now arise in relation to biometric data collected and stored by corporations. The discussion of Clearview AI in Chap. 3 is a case in point.

---

[1] Mariano-Florentino Cuéllar and Aziz Z. Huq review of Zuboff's Age of Surveillance Capitalism in *Harvard Law Review* vol. 133 2020 note 51 p. 1291) who reference in turn Cagan Urkup et al., Customer Mobility Signatures and Financial Indicators as Predictors in Product Recommendation, 13 PLOS ONE, July 2018, at 1, 2–5.

Social media is also analysed by law enforcement in liberal democracies. Predictive policing applies analytical techniques to identify likely targets in police investigations and allocate resources, including deriving intelligence from platforms such as Facebook and Instagram (Binder, 2016). As was discussed in Chap. 2, the use of social media in investigating the attack on the Capitol Building in January 2021 indicates how valuable it can be as a resource for law enforcement agencies. This is in spite of the fact that it is now well publicised since 2013 that law enforcement and security agencies are using social media resources extensively in their investigations and intelligence activities. The Snowden revelations provided evidence of a propensity for Western intelligence services to use this data on both individual and societal levels where it is relevant to their targets:

> The concept of surveillance is not unfamiliar in democratic states. The United States, The United Kingdom, and Australia are, for instance, continuously implementing additional surveillance infrastructures and legislatures, at the same time as prominent debates continue about citizen's privacy and rights in relation to their individual data… China's social credit system should be viewed as a warning to Western liberal democratic countries of what may be to come. As our technological age allows for vast amount of data to be collected from individuals across multiple platforms, integrated and used to construct representational profiles and map patterns and behaviours, as well as the continuous rating of others via rating applications, the digitising of identity and reputation is already well underway (Wang & Dobson, 2019, p. 228).

The biometric identification and data integration capabilities being utilised by China in the SCS are all available in liberal democracies, and are currently being used in a less systematic way. To date, China is the only country to have centralised and formalised a system that seeks to determine the value of an individual in a country and regulate their behaviour accordingly, using these capabilities; however, there is certainly the potential for this to occur in an incremental manner in countries around the world if steps are not taken to regulate these technologies more proactively with a view to preventing similar systems from being implemented gradually.

5.2.2 Technology-Based Regulation

Biometric technology is steadily becoming the main form of digital identity. Digital identity is vital to transacting in the online environment, where the majority of transactions will soon take place. As technology advances, the regulation of transactions through the use of technical system architecture is becoming an increasingly important addition to regulation using legislation and common law. Blockchain is a form of distributed ledger technology, with Bitcoin being the best known to date. Bitcoin facilitates peer-to-peer transactions, without the need for bank processing, using blockchain technology to record transactions and ownership. Bitcoin transactions are verified by other users of the network (Australian Government, 2020). Smart contracts are a more recent development of blockchain technology that enable legal contracts to be automatically executed by code to implement an agreement between parties, rather than being drafted on paper by a lawyer. Peer-to-peer networks validate conditions that initiate the automated execution of the contract. Rather than the contract being enforced by a court, the code written into the block chain guarantees the performance of the agreement (Governatori et al., 2018). Smart contracts prevent transactions taking place until a condition or threshold has been digitally validated, such as funds being transferred into an account. By contrast, traditionally hardcopy documents were signed as a means of verifying identity and signifying agreement. If a dispute occurred, legal recourse followed through the court system after a breach, and even then, would regularly be a matter of dispute, requiring significant amounts of time and money to be spent on legal representation in order to enforce it. Smart contracts therefore use technology to proactively prevent parties taking actions that are outside the terms of the contract–they are however, only as good as the data they rely upon.

Biometric identification is a means of validating identity that integrates effectively with these approach in an online environment, and will become increasingly used in this context. While a feature of bitcoin and blockchain to date is that they have bypassed government regulated sectors, such as banking and the legal profession, over time government infrastructure will likely be introduced to facilitate these transactions, and when that occurs, the government may have more, rather than less, control.

Regulatory theorists such as Joel Reidenberg and Lawrence Lessig have described the use of system architecture itself as an approach to regulation. Reidenberg uses the phrase *Lex Informatica* to refer to 'law' imposed by technological capabilities and system designs, rather than by legally proscribing activities by legislation:

> …law and government regulation are not the only source of rule-making. Technological capabilities and system design choices impose rules on participants. The creation and implementation of information policy are embedded in network designs and standards as well as in system configurations…the set of rules for information flows imposed by technology and communication networks form a *Lex Informatica* that policymakers must understand, consciously recognize, and encourage (Reidenberg, 1998, p. 553).

Lessig describes the interaction of system architecture with three other modalities: black letter law, social norms and market forces (Lessig, 1999; Miller, 2010). Regulators can use combinations of these to control activities, in both the real and digital contexts. For instance, law controls individual activities through the threat of legal sanctions, such as fines or imprisonment; supported by the market through pricing; stigma associated with illegal behaviour; and computer system architecture, such as a requirement that internet service providers block illegal websites. Acknowledging that online and digital environments are difficult to regulate–a regulatory framework, combining law with other modes, is necessary to be effective.

One advantage of system architecture based regulation is the high level of compliance, as circumvention usually requires advanced technical skills, can be efficient to implement because the private sector can be required to develop the infrastructure, and it does not take as long as enacting laws through parliament (although this raises questions of political accountability) (Lessig, 1999). Governments around the world are beginning to use these forms of regulation for new technologies such as blockchain and smart contracts that provide insights into the role that biometrics, big data, and algorithm-based decision making may have in the commercial sector in the future. It seems clear that biometrics will likely have an increasingly important role in identifying people transacting in online environments.

The establishment of system architecture to regulate smart contracts and digital currencies will provide the foundation for blockchain to become a mainstream part of the financial system in the future, providing authentication, security and auditability for digital currency transactions, and throughout the lifecycle of smart contracts. In late 2019, China announced it would launch its own cryptocurrency and associated infrastructure, setting out a timeline for this to take place over the years ahead (Cuthbertson, 2019). Western democracies, such as Australia are introducing similar approaches. A consortium between the government and private sector has begun work to establish an Australian National Blockchain (ANB) to enable businesses to digitally manage contracts, exchange information and conduct authentication:

> The ANB will allow organisations to digitally manage the lifecycle of a contract, not just from negotiation to signing but also continuing over the term of the agreement, with transparency and permissioned-based access among all parties in the network, by using blockchain-based smart contracts to trigger business processes and events. These contracts contain smart clauses which have the ability to record external data sources, such as Internet of Things (IoT) device data and self-execute if specified contract conditions are met (ANB, 2020).

Biometric identification can play an important role in the verification and security of online transactions involving smart contracts and bitcoin. It is likely that as biometrics becomes more widely used as an identifier, governments will need to provide central systems for the protection and verification of biometric profiles, rather than have them continue to be held in the various databases of private companies. In the same way that governments have seen the need to maintain infrastructure relating to smart contracts and bitcoin, in order for the commercial sector to have confidence in the technology, it is likely that will they will also recognise this need in relation to biometrics, as they become a proxy for identity in online transactions. In the light of concerns about corporations' misuse of personal data in general, and about the inability of governments effectively regulate technology corporations, this increased role of government would be welcome developments. However, it does now raise questions with respect to citizens' rights to their biometric data vis-à-vis governments. Part of the response to these questions might be the establishment of public sector organisations with relevant legislated authority over the storage and access to biometric data, e.g. statutory authorities, which are independent of both the private sector and governments.

5.3 Liberal Democracy

At various points in the discussions of biometric technology in this work we have invoked liberal democratic values, e.g. individual privacy/autonomy, and principles, e.g. freedom from interference from government if one has not committed a crime and is not reasonably suspected of having committed one, and done so in part because of the threat posed to liberal democratic values by biometric technology and big data, or, at least, certain uses of it (Miller, 2021; Miller & Bossomaier, 2021; Miller & Gordon, 2014). Moreover, we have provided ethical analyses of the uses for security purposes of particular biometric technologies, notably fingerprinting, facial recognition technology and DNA. Moreover, in the last chapter we discussed the integration of these technologies with non-biometric technologies. While space did not permit a comprehensive ethical treatment of these issues we did suggest that the problems needed to be framed, firstly, in terms of individual rights versus collective goods (Miller, 2010 Ch. 2) and, secondly, in terms of dual use dilemmas (Miller, 2018), i.e. roughly speaking, dilemmas arising because the use of these technologies has the potential to confer great benefits but also to impose great moral costs. In doing so we noted that the dual uses in question cut across the individual rights versus collective goods distinction since some of the uses of the technologies potentially benefited individual rights (e.g. right to personal security) and undermined collective goods (e.g. collective power of the citizenry in relation to the state). As we have just seen there is an emerging suite of second generation biometrics, e.g. gait analysis, cardiac activity. Each of these technologies and corresponding uses is in need of ethical analysis. However, as we have also just seen, while there is at this point in time inadequate ethically informed direction being given in relation to first generation and, more obviously, second generation biometrics, let alone the integration of biometric technologies with non-biometric technologies, there is one possible direction increasingly on display, namely, China's use of integrated biometric and non-biometric technologies to enable the realisation of its social credit system and, ultimately, to underpin an authoritarian state. There is also an increasing and somewhat alarming power imbalance within liberal democracies between technology corporations and individual citizens, and an accompanying inability of liberal democratic governments to address this imbalance.

The direction in which China is going is profoundly at odds with liberal democratic values and principles; indeed, it is entirely inconsistent with both of the pillars of liberal democracy, i.e. liberalism and democracy. Liberalism is committed to individual autonomy, i.e. freedoms of thought, speech, movement, assembly, etc., and entails significant limits on state power; democracy is committed to universal rights to vote and hold office, multiple political parties, free and fair elections, etc., and is inconsistent with an authoritarian state since in essence democracy entails government of the people, *by the people,* for the people. Moreover, liberal democracies seek to limit and dilute the power of the state by an assemblage of interrelated institutional arrangements and associated principles, including constitutions, the rule of law (as opposed to the rule of 'men'), separation of powers, (executive,

5.3 Liberal Democracy

legislature, judiciary), free and independent press, a free market and private ownership, including private ownership or, at least control, of personal data and, therefore, biometric data. Authoritarian states lack all or most of these institutional arrangements, or have them in name only or only to a limited degree.

That said, the contrast between contemporary liberal democracies, e.g. US, and some contemporary authoritarian states, e.g. Russia, should not be overstated. This is in part because there is at least one important feature of contemporary liberal democratic states which is evidently inconsistent with liberal democratic principles and, in particular, the autonomy of individual human beings, namely, powerful, hierarchically structured, private sector organisation, e.g. notably multinational corporations. Typically, most of the employees in these organisations have very little control over their actions qua employees which is to say over much of the activity they undertake during the course of their lives. In addition, as mentioned in earlier chapters, the customers of some of the largest of these corporations, e.g. the big tech companies such as Facebook and Apple, are subject to manipulation of a kind that compromises their autonomy, e.g. as a result of a business model according to which customers provide their personal data in return for the services provided rather than paying for them. More generally, private companies are by one means or another acquiring biometric data and using biometric technologies, e.g. Clearview's acquisition of billions of facial images scraped off the Internet and employment of facial recognition technology. We have argued that there can be adequate moral justifications for security agencies in liberal democratic states to use biometric technologies to provide the collective good of security if the use of these technologies is, for instance, necessary and proportionate, and if appropriate accountability mechanisms are in place. However, the use of biometric technologies by private companies for profit is an entirely different matter. Arguably, the use of facial recognition technology by private companies for profit, as in the case of Clearview, should simply be banned. In addition, speaking generally, biometric data should not be controlled by corporations; other more desirable institutional arrangements are possible such as, as mentioned above, storage of such data in organisations independent of corporations (and of governments and security agencies), e.g. statutory authorities. Here we need to distinguish between ownership of biometric data, storage of biometric data and access to biometric data. Depending on the biometric data in question, arguably, individual citizens should retain (defeasible) ownership rights over their biometric data, the independent authorities' should be granted storage rights in respect of this data (under restricted conditions) and security agencies granted rights of access to it (under warrant).

But to return to our larger canvas, China's social credit system conveniently illustrates a fundamental difference between liberal democracies and authoritarian states. The underlying assumptions of the social credit system are that the state ought to, firstly, determine what the collective good(s) of the citizenry are (in part, of course, by recourse to the uncontroversial de facto needs, such as food, clothing and shelter, of the citizens); secondly, determine what counts as being a good citizen, (e.g. someone who contributes to those collective goods but, in addition, who accepts the authority of the authoritarian state and complies with its laws, regulations and policies); and, thirdly, ensure that the citizens behave accordingly. In relation to the compliance of its citizens, China's embrace of biometric technology integrated with non-biometric technologies, has a crucial role to play (as described above). While liberal democratic states will inevitably embrace new and emerging technologies, including biometric technology, and the benefits they confer they must do so on their own terms, i.e. in a manner that does not undermine liberal democracy. By contrast with this authoritarian conception of the state, the liberal democratic state is not, or ought not to be, in the business of determining what are or are not the collective goods to be provided or what counts as a good citizen, and ensuring compliance with this model. Indeed, the reverse is the case; the citizenry ought to decide about these questions of collective goods and the state ought to enact its laws and frame its policies accordingly. Appropriately regulated, new and emerging technologies, such as social media, can facilitate liberal democracies by, for example, enabling large numbers of citizens to communicate with one another and leaders to communicate directly with citizens. Identification technologies, including biometrics, may well have a role to play here by, for example, ensuring that communicators are able to be identified and held accountable by those who they communicate with.

Moreover, if the government of the day fails to adequately represent its citizens or otherwise serve their collective interests, then, the members of the citizenry have the collective right (i.e. joint right (Miller, 2010 Ch. 2) – see Chap. 3 for discussion) to replace it via an election. Again, identification technologies, including biometrics, may have a role to play in relation to authenticating voters. And there is a further important point regarding the relationship of the individual to his or her fellow citizens in liberal democratic states.

Importantly, the rights of the individual (and of minorities) need to be protected from the tyranny of the majority and, more generally, from predatory groups. Here constitutions, such as the US constitution, have an important role to play, e.g. the right to free speech, as have law enforcement agencies impartially enforcing the law. In so far as new and emerging technologies, including biometrics, assist law enforcement agencies to impartially enforce laws that protect moral rights, these technologies should be embraced, as they largely have been, e.g. improved methods of fingerprinting and DNA.

However, in relation to the protection of the rights of the individual (and of minorities), including from the state and from the tyranny of the majority, the notion of freely undertaken joint action also has an important role to play, although this might at first seem counter-intuitive. Firstly, consider freedom of assembly, free and fair elections, and the moral rights to engage in these activities. These phenomena involve, we suggest, individuals freely undertaking *joint* action (Miller, 2010) (see Chap. 1 for discussion); one cannot participate in an assembly or an election on one's own. Moreover, and relatedly, these joint actions involve these individual freely exercising their joint rights (Miller, 2010 Ch. 2) (see Chap. 3 for discussion).

The enjoyment of rights is typically thought to be an individual affair; and indeed in many respects it is. If, for example, a person, A, has a right to individual freedom and it is fulfilled, then A enjoys the exercise of A's right and no-one else enjoys the exercise of A's right (even if, B for instance, enjoys the exercise of B's right). It is also true that the exercise of A's right to freedom is logically consistent with the inability of others to exercise their respective rights to freedom, e.g. if A is Robinson Crusoe living alone on an island cut off from civilisation and everyone else, i.e. B, C, D etc., lives in an authoritarian state.

It is a commonplace of political philosophy that the establishment of government and the rule of law is *instrumentally* necessary for the preservation of the freedom of each of us, albeit under the restriction not unduly to interfere with others; the alternative, as Hobbes famously said, is the state of nature in which life is nasty, brutish and short. However, we want to make a somewhat different point; there is another reason that most of us rely on the fulfilment of the rights to freedom of others in order to enjoy adequately our own freedom.

Specifically, person A cannot engage in (freely performed) *joint* activity with others, if these others cannot exercise their rights to freedom (Miller, 2010 Ch. 3). For example, A cannot freely participate in elections, unless others can also do so; hence the absurdity of A voting in an election in which all the other votes were cast in accordance with the instructions of the dictator of the country in question.

Indeed, joint action is (in part) constitutive of all institutions, political, economic and otherwise (Miller, 2010). Accordingly, unless A is the one, or one of the ones, who is in control of the actions of others – including determining their participation in joint activity – then A's freedom is (literally, and not merely figuratively) diminished to the extent that the freedom of others is. So the fulfilment of one person's right to freedom is importantly connected, directly or indirectly – via a pervasive network of joint institutional activity – to the fulfilment of the rights to freedom of many other persons. So the right to freedom of action, including freedom of assembly and freedom to vote in free and fair elections, are in part *joint rights* to engage in freely performed *joint action* (Miller, 2010 Chs. 2 & 3). Accordingly, to the extent that new and emerging technologies, such as social media, blockchain, identification technologies, and so on facilitate the exercise of joint rights to engage in joint activity that serves the collective ends of legitimate institutions, whether they be democratic governments, institutions of public communication, law enforcement agencies or financial institutions, then these technologies benefit rather than undermine liberal democracies.

5.4 Conclusion

As we saw in our discussions in previous chapters of existing biometrics and, especially, biometric and non-biometric integration, biometrics poses a series of dual use ethical dilemmas for liberal democracies. The same point holds even more in relation to future developments: biometrics has the potential to provide enormous benefits but also to cause great harm.

There are two aspects of future developments in relation to biometric identification that need to be considered. The first is new biometric technologies using unique physiological processes such as brain waves and cardiac rhythms that could provide greater accuracy and be more difficult to replicate. The second is the way that biometric data will change the governance of societies as it becomes the primary means of identity verification. The significance of the general points concerning joint action and joint rights in relation to political participation, and the potential facilitating roles of new and emerging technologies we have raised above, including to freely assemble and engage in free and fair elections, is as follows. Firstly, that the sharp contrast sometimes drawn between the two core components of liberal democracy, namely liberalism and democracy, is overdrawn. Properly understood, democracy is an expression of individual freedom, namely, freely undertaken joint action and, as such, stands in sharp contrast with authoritarianism.

Secondly, and relatedly, the sharp contrast that might be drawn between individual rights to freedom (e.g. privacy/autonomy) and collective goods facilitated by biometric identification (e.g. security) is overdrawn. For, at least in principle, citizens in a liberal democracy can freely (jointly) choose (directly or via their representatives) uses of biometric technologies that facilitate the collective good of security (and do so in a manner, at least in theory, consistent with preserving basic privacy rights, for example). If so, their rights to freedom are, at least to this extent, exercised rather than compromised. Naturally, if they make bad choices in this regard and, for instance, allocate too much surveillance power to the state and, thereby, jointly choose slavery (so to speak), then their individual rights to privacy/autonomy will be compromised – and perhaps also, via the increased power of the state, their freedoms in general. But this is far from inevitable; rather the collective (i.e. joint) decision is theirs to make.

Thirdly, liberal democracies commitment to individual autonomy and, as we are suggesting, the related value of freely chosen joint action, implies that reliance on widespread compliance with freely accepted, rationally-based, moral principles (e.g. principles of fairness) reinforced by social approval/disapproval, i.e. reliance on socio-moral norms, is to be preferred to reliance on compliance with top-down laws and regulations based on fear of punitive formal sanctions (such as the Social Credit System). Here we stress the freely accepted, rationally-based, moral dimension of the socio-moral norms in question, and also the fact that they are bottom-up. We note that new and emerging technologies can reinforce or undermine socio-moral norms; as mentioned above, it depends on how the technology is used, and by whom for what purpose. By contrast, authoritarian states prefer to rely on top-down laws and regulations based on fear of punitive sanctions and applied by authorities in the context of a state characterised by widespread use of surveillance technology and a docile, fearful population all too willing to report the 'transgressions' of fellow citizens to authorities. Importantly, for our purposes here and as we have seen, in contemporary authoritarian states the surveillance technology in question increasingly consists of biometrics technology integrated with non-biometric technologies such as smartphone metadata.

Fourthly, and relatedly, whether liberal democratic states retain their liberal-democratic character in the face of these technological and related developments depends on a number of factors. These include: (i) clear articulation and legal enshrinement of individual ownership rights to biometric data – including joint ownership rights in the case of genomic data – as distinct from the storage and access rights of governments, security agencies, statutory authorities and private sector organisations; (ii) clear articulation of, and compliance of governments, legislation and security agencies with, constitutive liberal democratic principles as they relate to biometric and other forms of identification technology, e.g. clear and significant limits on infringements of individual rights to privacy/autonomy, application of principles of necessity and proportionality to uses of new technologies, law enforcement accountability measures (e.g. use of judicial warrants), democratic accountability of governments, security agencies, laws, regulations and policies, e.g. via elected representatives and parliamentary committees but also privacy commissioners etc.; (iii) well-functioning, independent, epistemic (i.e. knowledge-based) institutions, e.g. statutory authorities to store biometric data, news media, universities (Miller, 2020); (iv) well-informed, rational and engaged citizenry (and the utilisation of well-regulated new and emerging technologies to achieve this); (v) an ability to embrace new and emerging technologies, such as biometric identification, in the service of individual and joint moral rights and liberal democratic institutions.

References

Armstrong, B., Ruiz-Blondet, M., Kahalifian, N., Kurtz, K., Jun, Z., & Laszlo, S. (2015). Brainprint: Assessing the uniqueness, collectability, and permanence of a novel method for ERP biometrics. *Neurocomputing, 166*, 59–67.

Australian Government. (2020). *National blockchain roadmap*. Department of Industry, Science, Energy and Resources.

Australian National Blockchain (ANB). (2020). *A new digital backbone for business*. https://www.australiannationalblockchain.com/

Bajwa, G., & Dantu, R. (2016). Neurokey: Towards a new paradigm of concealable biometrics-based key generation using electroencephalograms. *Computers and Security, 62*, 95–113.

Binder, C. (2016). Happenings foreseen: Social media and the predictive policing of riots. *Security and Peace, 34*, 242–247.

Chaurasia, P., Yogarajah, P., Condell, J., Prasad, G., McIlhatton, D., & Monaghan, R. (2015). Biometrics and counter-terrorism: The case of gait recognition. *Behavioural Sciences of Terrorism and Political Aggression, 7*, 210–226.

Chorzempa, M., Triolo, P., & Sacks, S. (2018). China's social credit system: A mark of progress or a threat to privacy? *Peterson Institute for International Economics Policy Brief 18-14*.

Cuthbertson, A. (2019, 30 October). China bans anti-blockchain sentiment as it prepares for launch of state cryptocurrency. *The Independent*. https://www.independent.co.uk/life-style/gadgets-and-tech/news/china-cryptocurrency-blockchain-bitcoin-a9176636.html

Dahlberg, L. (2015). Expanding digital divides research: A critical political economy of social media. *Communication Review, 18*, 271–293.

Danaher, J., et al. (2017). Algorithmic governance: Developing a research agenda through the power of collective intelligence. *Big Data & Society, July–December*, 1–21.

Galič, M., Timan, T., & Koops, B. J. (2017). Bentham, Deleuze and beyond: An overview of surveillance theories from the panopticon to participation. *Philosophy & Technology, 30*, 9–37.

Goffredo, M., Bouchrika, I., Carter, J., & Nixon, M. (2010). Performance analysis for automated gait extraction and recognition in multi-camera surveillance. *Multimedia Tools and Applications, 50*, 75–94.

Governatori, G., et al. (2018). On legal contracts, imperative and declarative smart contracts, and blockchain systems. *Artificial Intelligence and Law, 26*, 377–409.

Hambling, D. (2019, 27 June). The Pentagon has a laser that can identify people from a distance – By their heartbeat. *MIT Technology Review*. https://www.technologyreview.com/2019/06/27/238884/the-pentagon-has-a-laser-that-can-identify-people-from-a-distanceby-their-heartbeat/

Indumathi, T., & Pushparani, M. (2016). Automatic door opening using gait identification for movement as gesture. *Journal of Engineering Technology, 4*, 132–140.

Jolfaei, A., Wu, X., & Muthukkumarasamy, V. (2013). On the feasibility and performance of passthought authentication systems. In K. D. McDonald-Maier, G. Howells, & A. Stoica (Eds.), *IEEE computer society 2013 fourth international conference on emerging security technologies* (pp. 33–38). Conference Publishing Services.

Lessig, L. (1999). *Code and other laws of cyberspace*. Basic Books.

Miller, S. (2010). *The moral foundations of social institutions: A philosophical study*. Cambridge University Press.

Miller, S. (2018). *Dual use science and technology, Ethics and weapons of mass destruction*. Springer.

Miller, S. (2020). Freedom of political communication, propaganda and the role of epistemic institutions. In M. Christen, B. Gordjin, & M. Loi (Eds.), *Ethics of cybersecurity*. Springer.

Miller, S. (2021). Rethinking the just intelligence theory of national security intelligence collection and analysis: Principles of discrimination, necessity. *Proportionality and Reciprocity. Social Epistemology, 35*.

Miller, S., & Bossomaier, T. (2021). *Ethics and cybersecurity*. Oxford University Press.

Miller, S., & Gordon, I. (2014). *Investigative ethics: Ethics for police detectives and criminal investigators*. Blackwell.

Ngugi, B., Tarasewich, P., & Reece, M. (2012). Typing biometric keypads: Combining keystroke time and pressure features to improve authentication. *Journal of Organizational and End User Computing, 24*, 42–63.

Reidenberg, J. (1998). Lex informatica: The formulation of information policy rules through technology. *Texas Law Review, 76*, 553–593.

Revett, K., Deravi, F., & Sirlantzis. (2010). Biosignals for user identification: Towards cognitive biometrics? In G. Howells et al. (Eds.), *IEEE computer society 2010 conference on emerging security technologies* (pp. 71–76). Conference Publishing Services.

Rudrapal, D., Das, S., & Debbarma, S. (2014). Improvisation of biometrics authentication and identification through keystroke pattern analysis. In R. Natarajan (Ed.), *Distributed computing and internet technology: 10th international conference* (pp. 287–292). Springer.

Sıthigh, D. M., & Siems, M. (2019). The Chinese social credit system: A model for other countries? *The Modern Law Review, 82*, 1034–1071.

Smith, M., Mann, M., & Urbas, G. (2018). *Biometrics, crime and security*. Routledge.

State Council of the People's Republic of China (SCPRC). (2014, June 14). *Planning outline for the construction of a social credit system* (English translation: Creemer, R.). https://chinacopyrightandmedia.wordpress.com/2014/06/14/planning-outline-for-the-construction-of-asocial-credit-system-2014-2020/

Thaler, R., & Sunstein, C. (2009). *Nudge*. Penguin.

References

van den Hoven, J. (2008). Information technology, privacy and the protection of personal data. In J. van den Hoven & J. Weckert (Eds.), *Information technology and moral philosophy*. Cambridge University Press.

Wong, K., & Dobson, A. (2019). We're just data: Exploring China's social credit system in relation to digital platform ratings cultures in westernised democracies. *Global Media and China, 4*, 220–232.

Zuboff, S. (2019). *The age of surveillance capitalism*. Profile Books.

Open Access This chapter is licensed under the terms of the Creative Commons Attribution 4.0 International License (http://creativecommons.org/licenses/by/4.0/), which permits use, sharing, adaptation, distribution and reproduction in any medium or format, as long as you give appropriate credit to the original author(s) and the source, provide a link to the Creative Commons license and indicate if changes were made.

The images or other third party material in this chapter are included in the chapter's Creative Commons license, unless indicated otherwise in a credit line to the material. If material is not included in the chapter's Creative Commons license and your intended use is not permitted by statutory regulation or exceeds the permitted use, you will need to obtain permission directly from the copyright holder.

Index

A
Applied ethics, 7–9, 17
Artificial intelligence (AI), 33, 60, 75, 82
Australia, 5, 6, 22, 23, 27–29, 33, 49, 53, 58, 62, 63, 65, 67, 85, 87
Authoritarian governments, 70, 71, 73, 76
Autonomy, 14, 15, 29–32, 35, 41, 48–50, 52, 64, 68, 69, 74, 82, 88, 89, 92, 93
Avoidable outcomes of scientific research or technology, 73–74

B
Bhopal chemical disaster, 74
Big data, 48, 59, 64, 67, 81, 82, 87, 88
Biometric databases, 14, 17, 29, 59, 68, 70, 73, 81
Biometric identification, 1–4, 7, 14, 17, 35, 64, 75, 76, 79–82, 85–87, 92, 93
Border security, 32

C
Capitol Building riot, 28
Case of Gaughran v. The United Kingdom (Application no. 45245/15) ECtHR, 13 February 2020, 43
Case of S. and Marper v The United Kingdom ECtHR, 4 December 2008, 43
Chernobyl nuclear disaster, 74
Clearview AI, 27–29, 32, 35, 84
Closed circuit television (CCTV), 2, 14, 21, 22, 24–26, 28, 31, 33–36, 46, 61, 70, 73, 80, 82
Cognitive biometrics, 80

Collective ends, 10–14, 91
Collective goods, 8, 12, 15–17, 52, 68, 69, 88–90, 92
Collective responsibility, 9–11, 15, 39–53, 71
Consent, 5, 6, 16, 17, 22, 26–28, 32, 36, 45, 50–52, 59, 84
Contact tracing, 64, 65, 68
Coronavirus disease 2019 (COVID-19), 33, 64–68
Criminal investigations, 2, 9, 11, 13, 17, 21, 34, 39–41, 46, 47, 53, 57
Culpable negligence, 74

D
Data integration, 46, 59, 64, 85
Digital identity, 75, 85
Digitalisation, 3, 57
Digital templates, 22
Direct-to-consumer (DTC) genomics, 45
DNA database
    population wide DNA database, 41, 52, 74
DNA identification, 6, 17, 22, 23, 39–53, 82
DNA profiling, 2
Drivers licences, 23, 24, 33, 36, 41, 66, 67
Dual use dilemmas, 15, 69, 72–74, 88
Dual use science and technology
    definition of, 69–75

E
Encryption, 61–63, 68, 69, 73
Epistemic action, 75
Europe, 27, 42

F
Facial recognition, 2, 3, 14, 16, 17, 21–29, 31–36, 41, 43, 46, 61, 64–66, 68, 70–74, 80–83, 88, 89
Fingerprint identification, 2–7, 14, 17, 22, 57, 80
Forensic genealogy, 44–47
Forensic science, 6, 8
Fukushima nuclear disaster, 73, 74
Future biometrics, 79–87

G
Gain of function (GOF) research, 72
Gait analysis, 3, 80, 88
Genomic information, 44, 46, 52
Genomics, 41–53, 75, 93
Golden state killer, 46
Governance, 82, 83, 92

H
Hiroshima and Nagasaki, 70
Human Genome Project, 44

I
Identities, 2, 5, 6, 22, 24, 33, 34, 40, 49, 51, 58, 61, 64–67, 82, 85–87, 92
Interdependent action, 10

J
Joint actions, 10–13, 90–92
Joint epistemic action
Joint responsibility, 10–12, 52
Joint rights, 39–53, 90–92

L
Law
 criminal law, 48
 enforcement, 2, 3, 5–7, 9, 14–17, 23, 26–29, 31, 32, 35, 36, 41, 42, 44–53, 57–59, 61–64, 66, 68–71, 73, 74, 76, 82, 83, 85, 90, 91, 93
 evidence law, 7, 41
 law reform, 27, 76, 81
 legal systems, 8, 41
 legislation, 6, 23, 24, 36, 41, 42, 61–63, 85, 93
Liberal democracies, 29, 31, 34, 47, 48, 50, 53, 59, 66, 69, 76, 81–83, 85, 88–92

M
Metadata, 34, 46, 59–68, 70, 73, 75, 82, 83, 92
Moral responsibility, 9–17, 52–53, 68, 71
Moral rights, 15, 16, 30, 32, 34, 50–53, 69, 90, 93

N
National security, 5, 14–16, 25, 33, 36, 48, 61, 63, 64, 68, 69, 71
Nuclear fission, 73, 75
Nuclear science and technology

O
One-to-many searching, 2, 22, 24
One-to-one verification, 2
Online platforms, 83

P
Passports, 2, 3, 22–24, 28, 31, 32, 36, 41, 61, 66, 67, 70, 73
Personal identity, 30, 34, 35
Powers, 15, 25, 26, 31, 34, 43, 44, 48, 50, 53, 60, 69, 73, 83, 84, 88, 92
Privacy, 5, 7, 14, 15, 17, 25, 27–35, 41–44, 46, 48–50, 52, 53, 60, 63, 65, 68, 69, 73, 75, 76, 82, 84, 85, 88, 92, 93
Public safety, 25, 33–35, 48–50, 53

R
Regulations, 10, 23, 24, 26, 29, 32, 41, 44–46, 50, 53, 59, 60, 66, 69, 71, 75, 90, 92, 93
R (on the application of Bridges) v Chief Constable of South Wales Police (2020] EWCA Civ 1058, 26

S
Security, 5, 10, 12, 14–17, 23, 24, 28, 29, 31–36, 44, 47, 48, 50, 53, 58–60, 62, 64–76, 83–85, 87–89, 92, 93
Smartphones, 2, 3, 17, 61–66, 68, 75, 81, 92
Social credit system (SCS), 46, 59, 64, 81–83, 85, 88, 89, 92
Social media, 22, 27–29, 32, 59–61, 64, 66–67, 69, 70, 75, 83, 85, 90, 91
Surveillance, 22, 24, 25, 29, 31, 32, 34, 46, 48, 59–61, 64–66, 82, 85, 92

Index

System architecture (regulation), 82, 84–87

U
Union Carbide, *see* Bhopal chemical disaster
United Kingdom, 3, 5, 6, 22, 24, 26, 27, 29, 33, 41–43, 58, 85

United States, 3, 5, 22, 23, 27–29, 33, 42, 44–46, 49, 53, 58, 61, 62, 80, 85

V
Verification, 2, 22, 67, 87, 92